Je t'adore

W9-AUQ-068

Pepper Salt & Pepper Salt & Pepper Salt & Pepper

MENU DICTIONARY

GARÇON!

AGNEAU LAMB

ARTICHAUT ARTICHOKE
ASPERGE ASPARAGUS
AUBERGINE EGGPLANT

BARBUE BRILL FISH

BEARNAISE THICK YELLOW SAUCE WITH HERBS

BECASSE WOODCOCK

BEURRE BUTTER

BORDELAISE SAUCE WITH WINE AND MUSHROOMS

TARTE

SEL

CREVETTE SHRIMP

CROISSANT BREAKFAST ROLL

DINDON TURKEY COCK

ECREVISSES CRAYFISH

ESCARGOT SNAIL

FAISAN PHEASANT

FILET TENDER CUT OF MEAT OR FISH

FLAMBE FLAMING

FOIE GRAS GOOSE LIVER

FRAISE STRAWBERRY

FROMAGE CHEESE

GATEAU CAKE

MAIS CORN ON THE COB

MARENNES VARIETY OF OYSTER

MARRON CHESTNUT

MIEL HONEY

MOULE MUSSE

MOUTARDE M

NAVARIN

NOUILLE

OEUF

CAFETIERE

FROMAGE

FAISAN

SALADE

OIGNON

Handkerchiefs
A COLLECTOR'S GUIDE
Identification & Values

Helene Guarnaccia &
Barbara Guggenheim

COLLECTOR BOOKS
A Division of Schroeder Publishing Co., Inc.

COLLECTOR BOOKS
P.O. Box 3009
Paducah, Kentucky 42002-3009

www.collectorbooks.com

The current values in this book should be used only as a guide. They are not
intended to set prices, which vary from one section of the country to another.
Auction prices as well as dealer prices vary greatly and are affected by condition as well as demand. Neither the authors nor the publisher assumes respon-
sibility for any losses that might be incurred as a result of consulting this guide.

Searching For A Publisher?

We are always looking for people knowledgeable within their fields. If you feel
that there is a real need for a book on your collectible subject and have a large
comprehensive collection, contact Collector Books.

CONTENTS

DEDICATION

To our mothers,
Sylvia Guggenheim
and Essie Sulzer,
who wiped our tears,
waved us farewell,
and treated a cold
with hankies.
They set an example
for us to follow,
winding our way
through life,
hanky in hand.

A sweet wish with mother spelled out of ribbons.

A boxed set of hankies for your mother.

ACKNOWLEDGMENTS

A book is never written in a vacuum; there is usually inspiration and help from many sources. First and foremost, our "other halves" — Bert Fields (Barbara's husband), who doubled as editor, and Al Mackles (Helene's significant other), who had infinite patience with our never-ending search for wonderful hankies. We would also like to thank Ellen Baskin who helped with research; Matt Arigo and Logan Brown who kept order in the house; and Pamela Burton, a landscape architect, who identified species of plants that decorate the floral hankies. Joanne Dolan, a curator at the Fashion Institute of Technology, deserves our praise for her knowledge of the fabric designers of the period and for making FIT's collection of marvelous signed handkerchiefs available for our perusal. Lisa Stroup, Gail Ashburn, Beth Ray, and Amy Sullivan at Collector Books brought great enthusiasm to the project and wonderful eyes. Our photographers — Michael La Chioma, Joe Pugliese, and Jennifer Manley — made each image spectacular and a joy to behold. Finally, we would like to thank Jane Wyeth, a holiday hanky collector, who made her collection available to us, and Kathy Lautenschlager, whose hankies were so fabulous that it made us think: "They've got to be in a book!"

Think of Me.

Just a note to say... Thank You, © Welcher, $15.00 — 20.00.

ABOUT THE AUTHORS

Helene Guarnaccia has been interested in antiques for many years. When her children were young and she taught Spanish, she enjoyed going to antique shows and flea markets, furnishing her home in period items. In the 1980s, Helene became an antiques dealer and has written four books for Collector Books, which have sold over 100,000 copies. She lives in Fairfield, Connecticut.

Barbara Guggenheim has a doctorate in art history and is a well-known art consultant, lecturer, and contributor to *W* and other journals. By day, Barbara helps individuals and corporations purchase fine art, and by night and on weekends, she is a collectibles junky. She is passionate about her collections, which include handkerchiefs, salt and pepper shakers, Eiffel Towers, 1940s and 1950s tablecloths, lighthouses, ironstone, ceramic poodles, toothbrush holders, and others too numerous to mention!

INTRODUCTION

Handkerchiefs — taschentuchen, mouchoirs, fazzolettos, or panuelas — whatever they may be called — are a classic example of art expressed in a utilitarian object. Is "art" too pretentious a term? Would "kitsch" be more accurate? Perhaps, but it doesn't matter. These objects are amusing and attractive, while undeniably useful. But, really, would you blow your nose in the fanciful squares of cotton we've illustrated in this book? We hope not!

The hankies in this book date, for the most part, from the 1940s, 1950s, and early 1960s. With the invention of Kleenex in the 1920s, the hanky was considered unsanitary and unnecessary. During World War II, however, the hanky had a revival — not for its usefulness to stifle a cough or sneeze, but as a fashion accessory. With new advances in silk screening and color-fast dyes, bright, humorous, and brilliantly designed hankies replaced the dainty squares of white lace used earlier in the century. Hankies have always reflected the society in which they were made, but in the mid-century, more than ever before, they chronicled the changing mores, interests, and general mood of America.

Handkerchiefs are not new. They've been around in one form or another for thousands of years. Egyptians carried handkerchiefs as talismans. The Greeks and Romans wiped their faces with "handkerchiefs" woven of grass (ouch!). Handkerchiefs, as we know them, however, weren't commonly used until the late Middle Ages in Europe, when knights in armor tied their ladies' handkerchiefs to the back of their helmets. What lady would want to be without one lest she be asked for it by a handsome knight?

In the fifteenth century, far-sighted European traders brought back from China large quantities of peasants' headscarves, which equally far-sighted European women quickly appropriated as handkerchiefs. Because they were cheap and plentiful, their use spread widely throughout Europe. Soon they were made of linen, silk, and other fabrics. In 1480, Edward IV of England had dozens of handkerchiefs. History tells us that he died of a cold, after going fishing on a wet and chilly morning. If so, his handkerchiefs must have come in handy up to the bitter end.

By this time, the handkerchief began to serve other invaluable functions, apart from stifling a cough or sneeze. As personal hygiene and sanitary conditions left much to be desired, perfumed hankies were used to minimize odorous smells. With both men and women using handkerchiefs, they became a mode of non-verbal communication. A flourish in the right hands could punctuate conversation or send a message to an admirer across the room. Men and women gave small hankies (3" — 4" squares) to their beloved, which had button corners that kept the hankies in place in their hat bands for all the world to see. In the late sixteenth century, Elizabeth I had beautiful hankies encrusted with gold and silver. Hugely intelligent, a writer and linguist, she created and codified a vocabulary of gestures. A slight wave of her hanky and every experienced courtier knew it was time to leave the queen alone.

Handkerchiefs play more than a bit part in several of Shakespeare's plays. For the Bard, handkerchiefs were a character's personal symbol and a device to express emotion or heighten a scene without the need for dialogue. In *Cymbeline*, for example, the last we see of Posthumous as he sails away, having been banished by the king, is him waving and kissing his handkerchief to express his love for his wife, Imogen. In *As You Like It*, Orlando, wounded while saving his brother from a lioness, sends a hanky dipped in his blood to Ganymede (Rosalind dressed as a boy) to explain why he's late for their rendezvous.

In *Othello*, the devious Iago whips the great Moorish general into a jealous frenzy by telling him that Cassio was seen wiping his beard with a "handkerchief spotted with strawberries." The handkerchief had been given to Othello's mother by an Egyptian with the injunction never to part with it. According to the Egyptian, as long as his mother had it, his father would be in love with her. If she lost it or gave it away, her husband, Othello's father, would stray. Othello had given the handkerchief to his young, beautiful wife, Desdemona, with the same admonishment. Iago had planted the handkerchief on Cassio so that he could convince Othello that Desdemona had given it to the younger man and that they must be having an affair. Othello believed this and did what any husband would — he smothered Desdemona with a pillow. But Emilia, Iago's wife, confessed to Othello that she found the handkerchief in Desdemona's chamber and gave it to Iago, who had been urging her to steal it. Othello realizes he's been duped, but it's too late. Unable to un-smother Desdemona, he commits suicide as Iago is dragged off to be tortured. All because of a "strawberry spotted" hanky.

By the end of the seventeenth century, the number of handkerchief users mushroomed, as did the competition for bigger, flashier examples. The more intricate the hanky, the richer one was thought to be. Hankies ranged from plain unadorned linen, to silk or satin, with silver or gold thread encrusted with precious stones. Aristocrats sitting for their portraits often asked the artist to include a hanky as a symbol of wealth and class. Painters, such as Velasquez, were only too happy to accommodate, as the hanky provided a fine opportunity to demonstrate the artists' skillful brushwork.

Although many women embroidered or did the lace-work themselves, elaborate hankies could be purchased. Merchants were only too happy to regale buyers, as they are today, with tales of Venetian nuns who went blind making the very hanky they were trying to sell. Possibly the tradition of borrowing a bridal hanky was the result of the inability of young brides to afford expensive ones. With commercial, as well as sentimental value, hankies were handed down from one generation to another, even specifically bequeathed in wills.

Larger, darker colored hankies came into fashion for men who took snuff. The bigger the better, until things spun out of control. In 1785, Louis XVI, probably at the urging of Marie Antoinette, issued a decree standardizing a square format and prohibiting anyone from carrying a handkerchief bigger than his. Legend has it that a courtier was jailed for committing such an offense. A few years later, though the world changed politically, the hanky was still important. Napoleon, besotted by his wife, Josephine, carried her hanky on foreign campaigns, sniffing it and sighing at her scent.

Early settlers in America found imported handkerchiefs expensive until the cotton industry developed, and hankies were mass produced. To induce sales, manufacturers

printed hankies with illustrated political messages, history and spelling lessons. And if the hanky was big enough to be able to knot the corners together, it became a makeshift carryall.

By the turn of the last century, almost every man, woman, and child carried one, a practice which continued into the 1920s when Kimberly-Clark, a Wisconsin paper company, invented paper tissues. "Don't put a cold in your pocket" was their slogan that appealed to germ-phobic America. By the mid-1930s, hankies were all but gone, but not forever.

World War II changed everything. With their men away fighting, women entered the work force in large numbers for the first time. Housewives became Rosie the Riveter, working at men's jobs, earning men's wages. Now, women were controlling their own destinies — making decisions, buying the clothes they wanted — without having to ask permission. Besides, with all the men away at war, what was a girl going to do for fun other than flaunt a colorful themed hanky? Faced with the constant threat of death or devastating injury to husbands, brothers, and boyfriends, novelty hankies provided a needed lift for the spirits.

For many women, the fun was in having a whole wardrobe of hankies. They bought them to match every outfit, to celebrate holidays and occasions, or just because they were beautiful or fun. Handkerchiefs were the perfect accessory — they didn't go out of style and because they were inexpensive (from 15¢ up to $1.00), they provided the ideal solution for the woman "needing" a shopping fix. They also made great gifts — perfect for grandma or your child's teacher. Every woman could use a crisp, new handkerchief, whether she was large or small. With hankies, one size fits all! To make things easy, they were often sold in special gift cards, ready to sign and send.

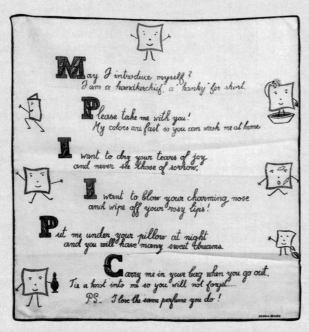

May I introduce myself? I am a handkerchief, a "hanky" for short.

Please take me with you! My colors are fast so you can wash me at home.

I want to dry your tears of joy and never see those of sorrow.

I want to blow your charming nose and wipe off your rosy lips!

Put me under your pillow at night and you will have many sweet dreams.

Carry me in your bag when you go out. Tie a knot into me so you will not forget....

P.S. I love the same perfume you do!

Hankies reflected the times and the new interests of women in society, like the ones with instructions on "how to catch a husband" or "how to mix the perfect martini," and the glamorous actresses of the period had a hand in getting out the message. When Bette Davis or Joan Crawford pulled a hanky from their sleeve (literally!), to wipe a tear or bid adieu, every woman in America left the theater inspired to do the same. Like Queen Elizabeth, women developed their own non-verbal hanky language, using gestures that their husband, lover, friends, and family would come to understand. Moreover, hankies provided a simple and accepted way to be pro-active in starting a relationship with a man. The perfect prop, dropped at the right moment in the path of a man you wanted to attract, went far to make him notice you.

By the late 1960s, women began once again to consider the hanky just as a utilitarian item, rather than a fashion statement. White linen squares replaced the storied hankies of the prior years. At about the same time, colorful hankies became popular in the gay community. Homosexuals, looking for action, would put a hanky in either rear pocket of their trousers. Its placement (left or right) and color signaled sexual preference. For example, if a man wanted to find a sex partner who'd assume a passive role, he'd wear a hanky in his right rear trouser pocket. If he himself wanted to be passive, he'd wear a hanky in the left pocket. It is still practiced to some extent, so if you see a man sporting a leopard-printed hanky in his left pocket? He's got tattoos. In his right pocket? He loves them.

What follows is just a sample of these remarkable, often silly, sometimes sentimental objects that so readily evoke a different time that was a watershed moment in our social history.

We hope that you enjoy looking at these marvelous objects as much as we have enjoyed collecting them. We've seen thousands and thousands, and just when we think we've seen them all, we find a new treasure. The variety is endlessly astounding — enough to blow your mind, if not your nose!

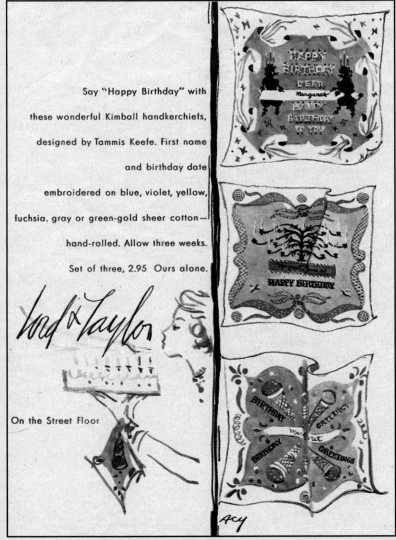

Lord and Taylor advertisement.

ANIMALS
Man's Best Friend & Others

"All animals are equal, but some animals are more equal than others."
George Orwell, *Animal Farm*, 1945, Chapter 10

With the rise of the middle class after World War II came the move to the suburbs. Couples purchased their own homes and started having children. Americans embraced the idea that no family was complete without pets. Dry dog foods began to be manufactured, making it even easier to care for your dog. Programs on TV extolled animals, like *Lassie* and *Mr. Ed*, which left us with indelible images of a loyal, courageous dog and a talking horse. Whether they're shown as specific breeds or generic, rendered realistically, stylized, or in a comic book fashion, animals have a high lovability factor.

Adoring poodle couple,
Franshaw, paper label. $15.00 — 20.00.

Head shots of two poodles —
one black, one white. $10.00 — 15.00.

A trio of posing poodles on green ground,
manufactured by Skandia. $15.00 — 20.00.

Poodle in a basket — French poodles
like all things French, were admired in
America after World War II. $10.00 — 15.00.

Frolicking poodles, by Hazel Ware. $15.00 — 20.00.

Oodles of poodles. $5.00 — 10.00.

Coiffed poodles with pink bows, by
Kit Ann, Lady Heritage label. $15.00 — 20.00.

Pink poodle and friends,
by Tammis Keefe. $30.00 — 40.00.

Poodles canoodling, by Hazel Ware. $15.00 — 20.00.

A tableau of dogs, by Tammis Keefe. $35.00 — 40.00.

Lonesome Scottie. $10.00 — 15.00.

Cocker sipping tea, manufactured by Burmel. $2.00 — 25.00.

Bulldog putting on the dog,
manufactured by Burmel. $20.00 — 25.00.

Soda fountain dachshund,
manufactured by Burmel. $20.00 — 25.00.

Frolicking poodles, fabulous design by Carl Tait. $40.00 — 45.00.

Graphic Dalmatians and others, by Tammis Keefe. $30.00 — 35.00.

A naughty cocker waits to get caught. $6.00 — 10.00.

Blue-eyed kittens, a Skandia print, 1967 — 1968, made in Switzerland. $12.00 — 15.00.

Green-eyed kittens and kitty close-up against a green background. $10.00 — 12.00.

Kittens playing with yarn, by Frederique. $15.00 — 20.00.

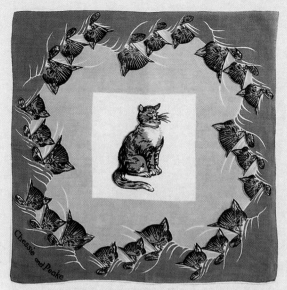

Chessie and Peake. In the 1930s these two were mascots for the C&O Railroad. $30.00 — 35.00.

Kitten and yarn, Lady Heritage label. $15.00 — 20.00.

Inquisitive kitten. $8.00 — 10.00.

Japanese style fat cat. $8.00 — 12.00.

Tammis Keefe's kitties and cats. $30.00 — 35.00.

Proud horses in a traditional,
photographic style. $8.00 — 12.00.

Kangaroo mother and joey with
umbrellas, by Don. $15.00 — 20.00.

Announcing the newest arrivals, by Kati. $20.00 — 25.00.

Rooster, by Faith Austin, manufactured by
Franshaw exclusive, paper label. $20.00 — 25.00.

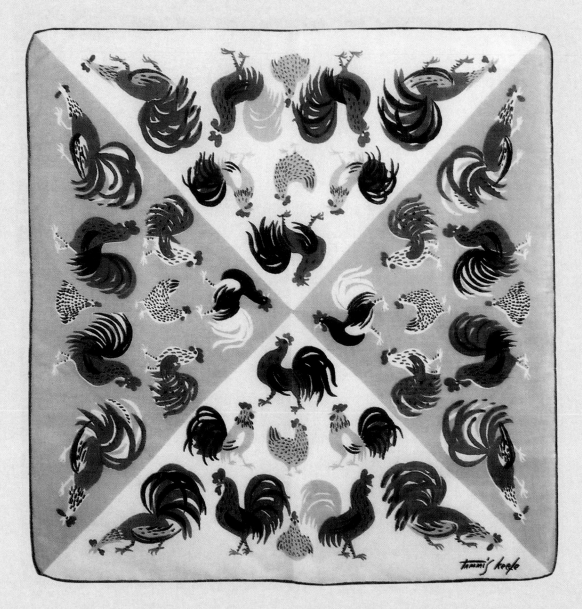

Roosters and hens in quadrants, by Tammis Keefe. $30.00 — 35.00.

Woeful pink lions, by Erin O'Dell, with paper price sticker "T.A. Chapman" on reverse, 69¢, 3 for $2.00. $25.00 — 30.00.

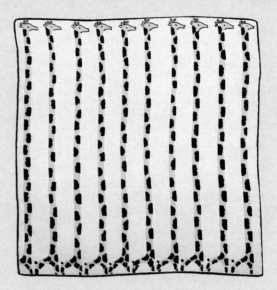

Very long-necked giraffes. $15.00 — 20.00.

A quartet of roosters, by Peg Thomas. $8.00 — 12.00.

Red and white and striped all over (a play on "What's black and white and read all over"). $15.00 — 20.00.

Big game trophy heads, by Tammis Keefe. $40.00 — 45.00.

Whoo's there? Owls perched in tree branches with a twist, by Tammis Keefe. $30.00 — 35.00.

Penguins — not in black tie!, by Tammis Keefe. $30.00 — 35.00.

Donkeys, carts, and swags. $8.00 — 12.00.

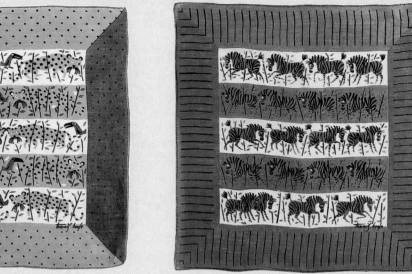

Leopards camouflaged in grass,
by Tammis Keefe. $30.00 — 35.00.

Zebras, by Tammis Keefe. $35.00 — 40.00.

Who belongs to whom?, by Tammis Keefe. $30.00 — 35.00.

Chirping birds announce spring. $5.00 — 10.00.

DESIGNER
Art for Art's Sake

Ars Gratia Artis

Several hanky artists were well-known designers of textiles. The best known was Tammis Keefe, who, as well as working under her own name, worked pseudonymously under the name Peg Thomas. As most hankies only cost between 15¢ and $1.00, women waited for the next designs from their favorite artist to come on the market. Carl Tait, Pat Prichard, Jeanne Miller, and Tom Lamb are other well-collected designers.

The circus had wide appeal in the years after the war, with traveling big tops delighting kids all over the country. The circus had roots in traditional art. Picasso, for example, repeatedly painted acrobats and other performers. Even before him, artists identified with circus performers — admiring their pure, if not tragic, lives — traveling from one place to another, living only for their art.

Tammis Keefe takes on Persian manuscripts. $30.00 — 40.00.

Conversations in Persian taste,
by Tammis Keefe. $30.00 — 35.00.

Polo player encircled by leopard spots,
by Tammis Keefe. $30.00 — 35.00.

Carousel horses, by Tammis Keefe. $30.00 — 35.00.

Under the big top, by Tammis Keefe. $30.00 — 35.00.

Tight-rope-walking poodles,
by Tammis Keefe. $30.00 — 35.00.

Acrobats, by Tammis Keefe. $40.00 — 45.00.

Harlequins, by Tammis Keefe. $40.00 — 45.00.

Ringmaster leads a four-ring circus,
by Tammis Keefe. $40.00 — 45.00.

Hoisting the sails, by Tammis Keefe. $40.00 — 45.00.

Royal procession, by Tammis Keefe. $40.00 – 45.00.

Tea sipping dragon sits it out!, by
Tammis Keefe. $30.00 – 35.00.

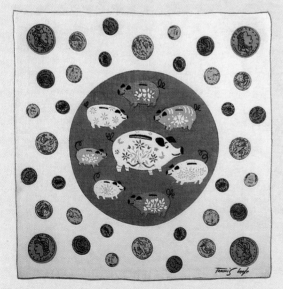

These little piggies help you save for a
rainy day, by Tammis Keefe. $40.00 – 45.00.

Dragonflies on striped background,
original Kimball label. $40.00 – 45.00.

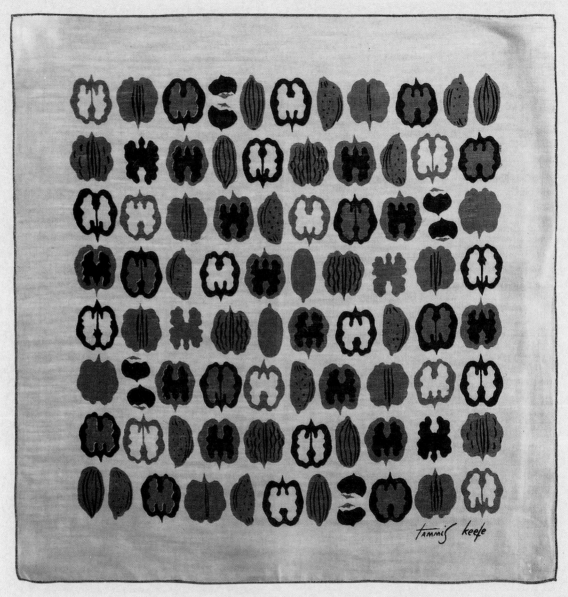

Walnuts or Rorshach?, by Tammis Keefe. $35.00 — 40.00.

Scarecrows and sunflower,
by Tammis Keefe. $35.00 — 40.00.

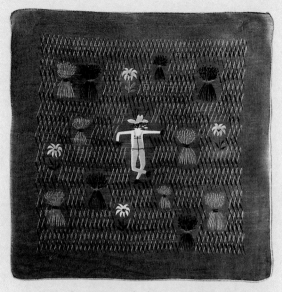

Scarecrow and wheat stacks, by
Tammis Keefe. $35.00 — 40.00.

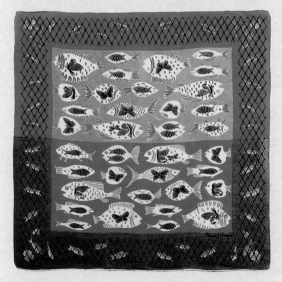

Something's fishy, by Tammis Keefe. $40.00 — 45.00.

Weather vanes and ornamental figures surrounding
a pile of umbrellas, by Tammis Keefe. $30.00 — 35.00.

Early American artifacts, by Tammis Keefe. $30.00 – 35.00.

Please take a seat!, by Tammis Keefe. $30.00 – 35.00.

A quartet of Barbershop poles,
by Tammis Keefe. $30.00 – 35.00.

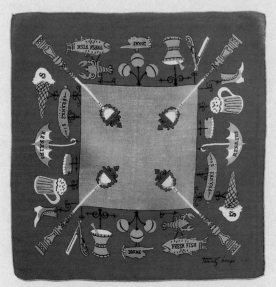

Gay nineties lamp posts and shop
signs, by Tammis Keefe. $30.00 – 35.00.

Hot air balloons, by Tammis Keefe. $45.00 – 50.00.

Camels at the oasis, by Peg Thomas. $12.00 — 15.00.

Sophisticated classical fret motif,
by Faith Austin. $25.00 — 30.00.

Butterflies in a field of clover,
by Faith Austin. $30.00 — 35.00.

Bunches of grapes, by Faith Austin,
original label. $15.00 — 20.00.

Billie Kompa's view of underwater life. $15.00 — 20.00.

Sea creatures, by Billie Kompa. $15.00 — 20.00.

Autumn leaves, by Dwaine Meek. $12.00 – 18.00.

Flowered plaques, by Jeanne Miller. $8.00 – 12.00.

Colorful kitties at play, by Hazel Ware. $15.00 – 20.00.

Autumn Harvest, by Sally Victor,
a famous hat designer. $10.00 – 15.00.

Signs of autumn, by Carl Tait. $40.00 — 45.00.

Jeanne Miller's hanging lanterns. $15.00 — 20.00.

Cats and dogs, by Pat Prichard. $8.00 — 12.00.

Not playing with a full deck, by Pat Prichard. $12.00 — 18.00.

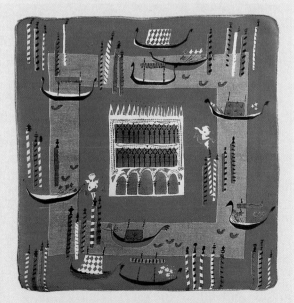

Gondolas, by Pat Prichard. $30.00 — 35.00.

FOOD
Eat, Drink & Be Merry

"It's food too fine for angels."
Edward Taylor, *Sacramental Meditations*

With the rise of the middle class and the increase in leisure time, Americans wanted to entertain in their new homes. Looking for a little sophistication, they readily embraced exotic recipes which made their way to America from all parts of the world. There were fondue parties, and spaghetti and pizza were served at home and at restaurants everywhere. Barbecues and casual meals shared by families and their neighbors became an American institution, along with square dances, luaus, and other theme parties.

Salt and pepper — variations on a popular table item. $10.00 — 15.00.

Barbecue — too cute to clean up sticky fingers. $40.00 — 45.00.

Trompe l'oeil lobster, by Tammis Keefe. $30.00 — 35.00.

The soda fountain became the place for teenagers to meet. $30.00 — 40.00.

La Fondue (in French) — a perennial French favorite. $40. 00 — 45.00.

Swiss Air menu. Many airlines presented travelers in first class with handkerchiefs on which the menu was printed. $10.00 — 15.00.

Easy-to-follow recipe for crepes Suzettes, if you can read French, that is. $50.00 — 55.00.

Spaghetti — everybody's favorite Italian food. $40.00 — 45.00.

Tea for Two — Frederique's sophisticated color combination complements the perfect afternoon respite. $10.00 — 15.00.

Fondue, by Kreier, another take on the "in" party snack. $40.00 — 45.00.

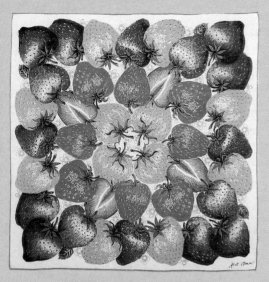

Luscious strawberries fill the
field, by Kit Ann. $15.00 — 20.00.

Kreier's geometric approach to
salad fixings. $10.00 — 15.00.

An old-fashioned general store in
up-to-date colors. $10.00 — 15.00.

Calories and vitamins. The calorie counts are faded.
Is that good or bad news? Fitness became important
to Americans as sports gained in popularity. $15.00 — 20.00.

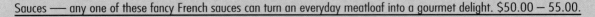
Sauces — any one of these fancy French sauces can turn an everyday meatloaf into a gourmet delight. $50.00 — 55.00.

Calories chart, the town "Kreier" applies the calorie count to some fancy foods. When it comes to caviar, who's counting. $20.00 — 25.00.

Easy-to-carry, calorie-counting cheat sheet. $10.00 — 15.00.

A full day's calorie count according to Phila Webb, in free-hand painterly approach. $20.00 — 25.00.

Preside over cocktail hour by mixing any of these libations. $40.00 — 45.00.

When he is the cook, some things never change. $40.00 — 45.00.

With these seven cocktail recipes, you'll not be bored all week. $25.00 — 30.00.

Cocktail recipes — some of these popular post-war drinks are making a twenty-first century comeback. $25.00 — 30.00.

Cocktails with an international flair. $25.00 — 30.00.

This hanky whimsically offers cocktails… with a tomato juice chaser, dessin depose (drawing registered) lower right. $25.00 — 30.00.

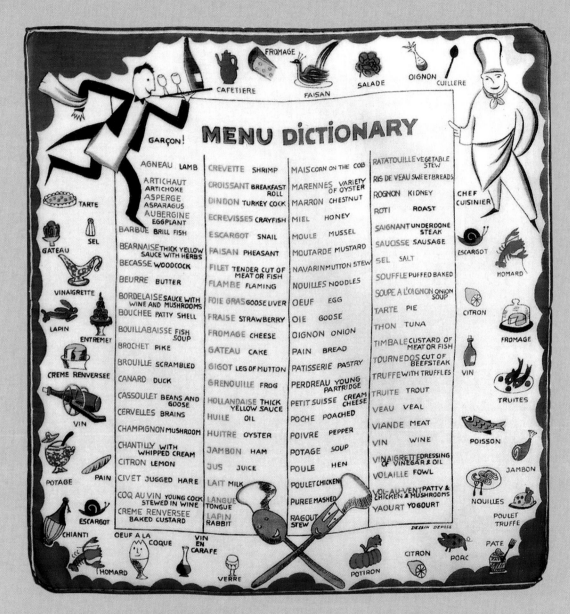

Menu dictionary — French with English translation. Take this with you on your next trip to France, and you can order like a native. $40.00 — 45.00.

A toast in any language. $30.00 – 40.00.

An easy guide to everybody's favorite bubbly, champagne, including the best dates. $40.00 – 45.00.

When Irish eyes are smiling, it's time for an Irish coffee. $20.00 – 25.00.

An assortment of liquor labels from French cointreau to Canadian whisky. $15.00 – 20.00.

Fine dining superstitions in English and French. $30.00 — 40.00.

Cocktail recipes bordered by fruit. The after-work cocktail hour became an institution in the 1950s, whether to meet friends at a bar or go home for a martini was the thing to calm you down after a hard day at the office. $30.00 — 35.00.

LIFE
Love, Luck, and Fun & Games

"In short, luck's always to blame."

Jean de La Fontaine

With hankies used to express love, the variety is not surprising. Along with love, chance and luck figure strongly in getting the best out of life.

Sports was the glue that helped keep our country together during World War II, keeping spirits high. After the war, people took up tennis, riding, swimming, and fishing, and spectator sports took hold like never before. Nothing could beat taking the kids to the ball game.

The building blocks of love. $20.00 — 25.00.

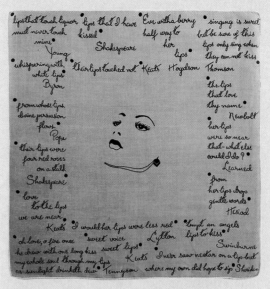

Lines about lips from famous poems and plays. $40.00 — 45.00.

Famous lovers through history. Can you guess who's who? Starting with Adam and Eve. $10.00 — 15.00.

Ooh la la! "Prends garde au loup" means "Beware of the Wolf" (a popular French song of the day). $10.00 — 15.00.

What to buy as an anniversary gift from the first anniversary to the seventy-fifth. $10.00 – 15.00.

I looked at you and time stood still, a corny
but timeless sentiment. $15.00 — 20.00.

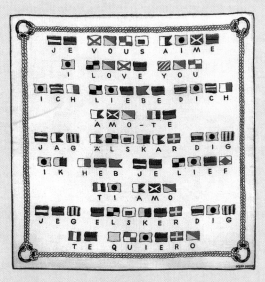

The international language of love. In words or semaphore,
the message is the same in any language. $40.00 — 45.00.

Sharing a soda, can a first
kiss be far behind? $10.00 — 15.00.

The daisies say it in French in all
ranges of emotion. $20.00 — 25.00.

EPINGLEZ CE MOUCHOIR A UN MUR SOUS UN BON ECLAIRAGE . A 5 METRES VOUS DEVEZ POUVOIR LIRE DE CHAQUE ŒIL LA PREMIERE LIGNE.

SINON VISITEZ UN OPTICIEN......... ET UN SPECIALISTE DU CŒUR !

PIN UP THIS HANDKERCHIEF TO THE WALL UNDER A GOOD LIGHT. 5 YARDS AWAY YOU MUST READ EASILY WITH EACH EYE THE FIRST LINE

OTHERWISE SEE YOUR OPTICIAN......... AND A HEART SPECIALIST !

A Mondrian-like eye chart with the test of letters spelling out
"I love you" in English and French, dessin depose. $40.00 — 45.00.

Carl Tait takes on the simple rhyme that says so much. $40.00 – 45.00.

Carl Tait's interpretation of "the report" (Kinsey?) with whimsical images translating hard scientific data. $35.00 – 40.00.

Cross-cultural good luck symbols. $30.00 – 35.00.

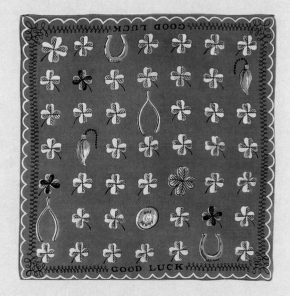

Lucky charms. $15.00 – 20.00.

Of all the rotten luck. $40.00 — 50.00.

Superstitions and symbols of luck, both good and bad. $25.00 — 30.00.

More warnings and omens for good and bad luck. $20.00 — 25.00.

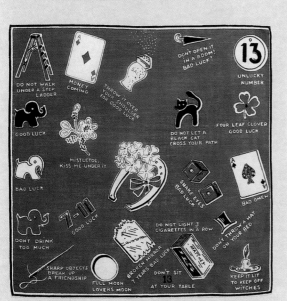

Third time's the charm. $20.00 — 25.00.

Lucky numbers and symbols. $15.00 — 20.00.

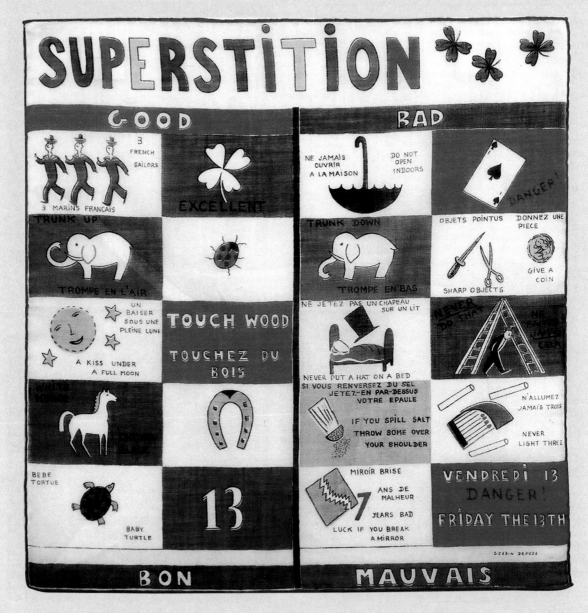

Good and bad superstitions in English and French, dessin depose. $50.00 – 55.00.

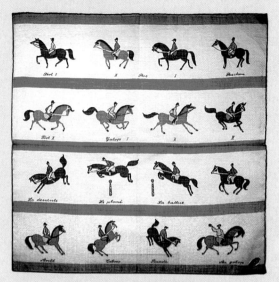

Putting a horse through his paces,
the French way. $20.00 — 25.00.

Equestrian, image of horse's head and
other riding gear. $20.00 — 22.00.

Equestrians in traditional style,
surrounding a horse's head. $20.00 — 22.00.

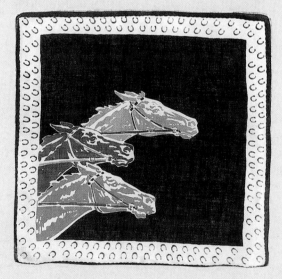

And the winner by a nose. $8.00 — 12.00.

Famous horse races around the world, dessin depose. $20.00 — 25.00.

Take me out to the ball park,
by Tammis Keefe. $45.00 — 65.00.

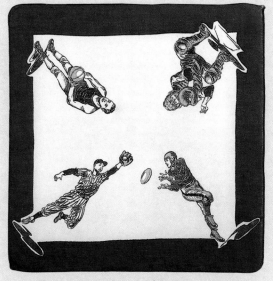

Three seasons of sports. $10.00 — 12.00.

Golf courses on Long Island, by
Tammis Keefe. $30.00 — 35.00.

Time to tee off! $35.00 — 45.00.

Setting sail with a sophisticated design. $10.00 — 15.00.

Tennis anyone? She's a tad
overdressed, no? $15.00 — 20.00.

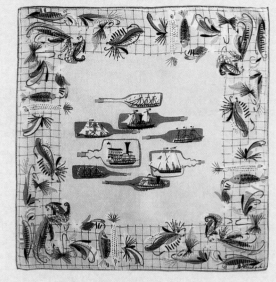

Ships in bottles and fishing lures make
a lively Pat Prichard design. $15.00 — 20.00.

Ski poles and gloves punctuate a snow
scene, by Tammis Keefe. $30.00 — 35.00.

Football players on the yard lines. $20.00 — 25.00.

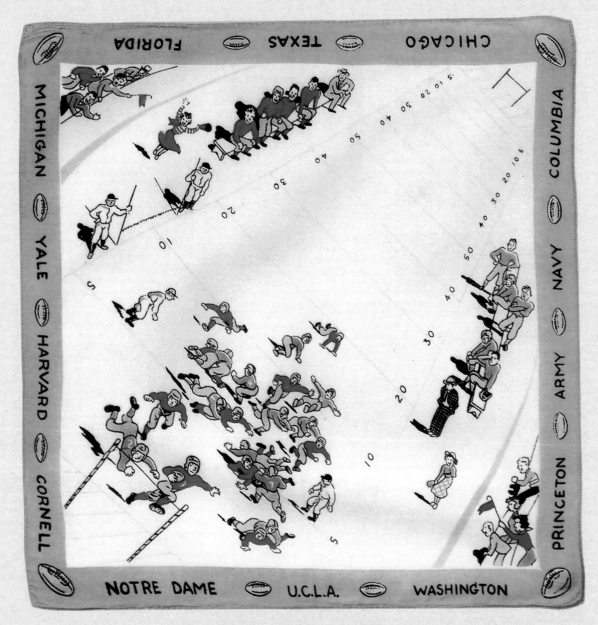

College football. $20.00 — 25.00.

Sports for all seasons. $15.00 — 20.00.

The joker is wild — and surrounded
by all four suits. $20.00 — 25.00.

Lucky in love, unlucky at cards,
by Pat Prichard. $50.00 — 55.00.

Canasta — everyone's favorite card
game in the 1950s. $10.00 — 15.00.

Optical chess. $20.00 — 25.00.

Canasta (canasta means "basket" in Spanish). $20.00 — 25.00.

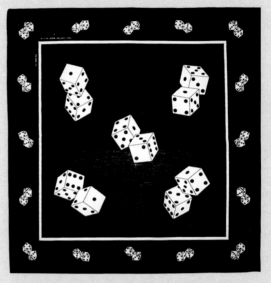

Lucky sevens in black and white. $10.00 — 15.00.

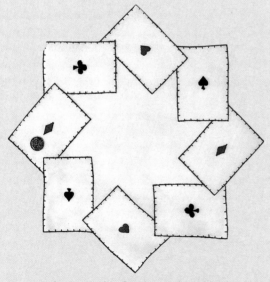

Eight aces embroidered on a shaped hanky, paper label, made in Switzerland. $10.00 — 15.00.

A roll of the dice. In French, "Chance et bonheur!" In English, "Luck and happiness!" $15.00 — 20.00.

OCCASIONS
Holidays, Greetings, Proverbs & Other Words of Wisdom

"Patch griefs with Proverbs."
William Shakespeare, *Much Ado About Nothing*, Act V, Scene 1

With the commercialization of holidays, the hanky found itself in the fray. They were made for almost every occasion, and today there are collectors so specialized, that they collect only holiday-themed handkerchiefs.

Ring in the New Year with this
Pat Prichard design. $20.00 — 25.00.

Which key will open the lock to your heart? $10.00 — 15.00.

White on red makes for a powerful design. $5.00 — 10.00.

Lively and happy sentiment. $4.00 — 8.00.

Romeo Juliet ♥ Psyche Cupid

Orpheus Eurydice ♥ Ramona Alessandro

Tristan Isolde ♥ Antony Cleopatra ♥ Pygmalion

Galatea ♥ Daphne Apollo ♥ Helen Paris – Menelaus

♥ Hamlet Ophelia ♥ Nanki-Poo Yum-Yum ♥ Ulysses

Penelope ♥ Dante Beatrice ♥ Launcelot Elaine ♥

Echo Narcissus ♥ Hiawatha Minnehaha

Daphnis Chloe ♥ Abelard Heloise ♥ John

Priscilla ♥ Robin Hood Maid Marian

Napoleon Josephine ♥ Harlequin

Columbine ♥ Enid Geraint

Evangeline Gabriel

Venus Adonis

Famous couples fill the heart with love. $15.00 – 20.00.

Nothing square about a lot of hearts. $8.00 — 12.00.

Hearts in dainty floral pattern. $5.00 — 8.00.

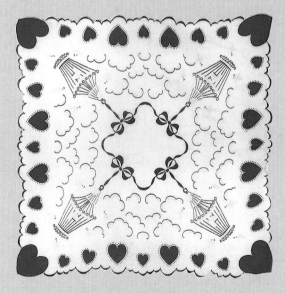

Hearts and lovebirds in cages. $3.00 — 8.00.

Cupid at work and play. $3.00 — 8.00.

Hearts and flowers. $3.00 — 8.00.

Silhouettes of hearts. $3.00 — 8.00.

A whoosh around hearts. $3.00 — 8.00.

A circle of hearts. $3.00 — 8.00.

A few shots from Cupid's bow
hit their mark. $20.00 — 25.00.

Always in my heart, I love you, in heart-shaped scallops. $8.00 — 12.00.

View of several hearts. $5.00 — 10.00.

Valentine's concentric hearts. $5.00 — 10.00.

Shamrocks to spare. $8.00 — 12.00.

Lucky four-leaf clover. $8.00 — 12.00.

Reversed pattern of clovers in the border for a lively composition. $5.00 — 10.00.

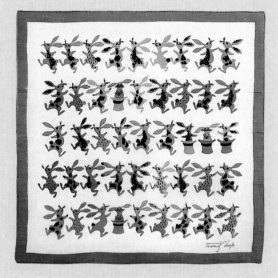

Hippity-hoppity, Easter's on its way, by Tammis Keefe. $30.00 — 35.00.

Have an "eggs"cellent Easter, by Tammis Keefe. $35.00 — 40.00.

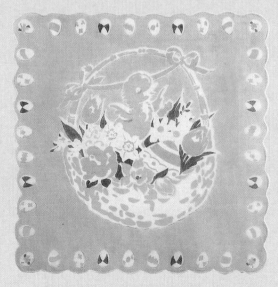

Easter basket with chicks. $3.00 — 8.00.

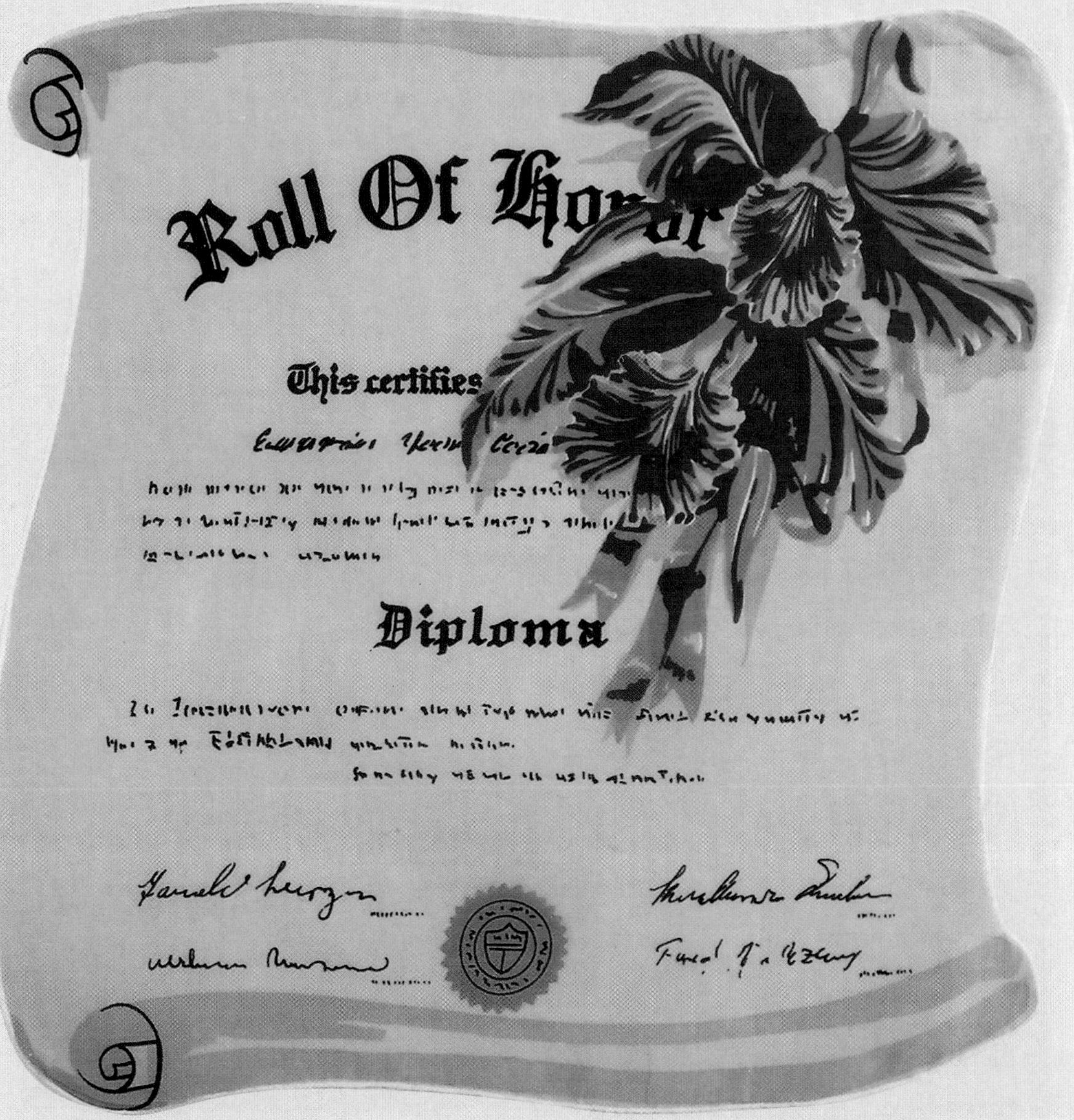

Pomp and circumstance in the shape of a sheepskin. $15.00 – 20.00.

Here comes the bride! $10.00 — 15.00.

Carl Tait sends musical greetings
for a happy birthday. $40.00 — 45.00.

1960s kitsch says it with flowers. $3.00 — 8.00.

Happy birthday and joyeux
anniversaire (French). $15.00 — 20.00.

Carl Tait gets festive with this feminine happy birthday hanky. $40.00 – 45.00.

This happy birthday hanky takes the cake. $15.00 — 20.00.

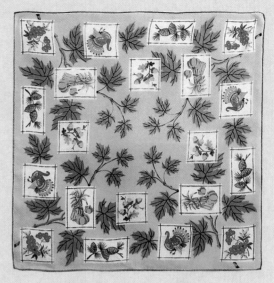

Turkeys and autumn foliage
signal Thanksgiving. $15.00 — 50.00.

Turkeys on the fence. $15.00 — 20.00.

Home at Christmas, by Tammis Keefe,
also signed A. Gilbert. $20.00 — 25.00.

Santa and Rudolf take off, by Carl Tait. $40.00 — 45.00.

Carl Tait spells out season's greetings
with Christmas stockings. $40.00 — 45.00.

A colorful assortment of holiday
greetings, by Carl Tait. $40.00 — 45.00.

Tammis Keefe spreads holiday cheer
on a field of snowflakes. $25.00 — 30.00.

Mountain village snow scene, in style of
a woodcut, by Kreier. $15.00 — 20.00.

Jingle bells ring in the season. $15.00 — 20.00.

Reflecting Santas, by Tammis Keefe. $30.00 — 40.00.

Reindeer prances on candy canes. $10.00 — 15.00.

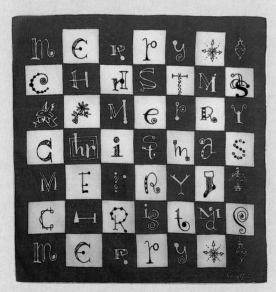

A checkerboard Merry Christmas,
by Chuck Green. $20.00 — 25.00.

Noel tree ornaments. $20.00 — 25.00.

Silent Night, a Christmas classic. $10.00 — 15.00.

Santa and reindeer in bright holiday green
and red, by Tammis Keefe. $30.00 – 35.00.

Tammis Keefe's Noel. $30.00 – 35.00.

Angels decorating a tree. $15.00 – 20.00.

Tree ornaments, by Hazel Ware. $15.00 – 20.00.

A stylish arrangement of holiday greetings. $15.00 — 20.00.

Holly decks the halls. $5.00 — 10.00.

Santas on skis, by Tammis Keefe. $40.00 — 45.00.

Santas and reindeer, by Tammis Keefe. $40.00 — 45.00.

Christmas hanky in a card. $5.00 — 10.00.

Poinsettias signal Christmas joy. $3.00 — 5.00.

A Merry Christmas, candles aglow, © Welcher. $15.00 — 20.00.

Bon voyage, have a heavenly trip, © Welcher. $15.00 — 20.00.

A nosegay on this happy day, © Welcher. $15.00 – 20.00.

Your birthday, that's a horse of a different color, © Welcher. $15.00 — 20.00.

Bringing you lots and lots of birthday wishes, © Welcher. $15.00 — 20.00.

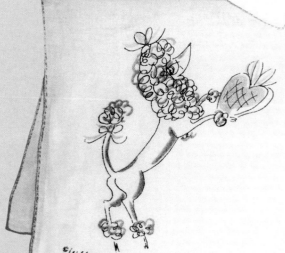

Je t'adore every birthday, more and more, © Welcher. $15.00 — 20.00.

For an elegant birthday simply go out and raise a little hell. $15.00 — 20.00.

Sick? Get well quick, © Welcher. $15.00 – 20.00.

Hazel Ware's poodles offer oodles
of thanks for your party. $15.00 – 20.00.

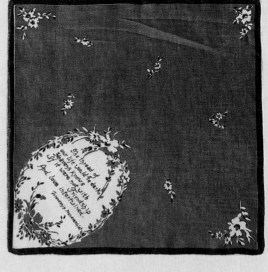

Poem for friendship. $6.00 – 10.00.

A toast to friendship. $6.00 – 10.00.

Good luck wishes for getting well soon,
by Tammis Keefe. $10.00 – 15.00.

A tic-tac-toe of illustrated proverbs. $15.00 — 20.00.

Half words, half pictures get the message
"A bird in the hand" across. $15.00 – 20.00.

Make hay while the sun shines in words
and pictures, by Carl Tait. $40.00 – 45.00.

Rich man, poor man and a twist on other
career choices, by Carl Tait. $40.00 – 45.00.

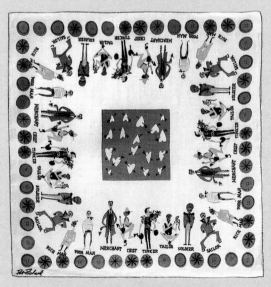

Pat Prichard's variation on the rich man,
poor man theme. $15.00 – 20.00.

HOROSCOPES & CALENDARS
Signs of the Times

"If thou follow thy star, thou canst not fail of a glorious haven."
Dante Alighieri, *The Divine Comedy, Inferno*

Because calendars are dated, it's easy to chronicle the changes in hanky design over a twenty year period. The more complex designs of the 1940s and 1950s gave way to simpler designs in the 1960s, when hankies finally fell out of favor.

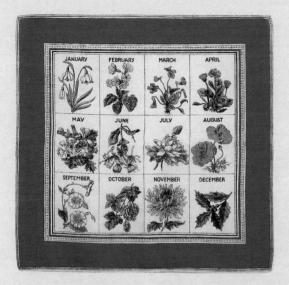

Flowers of the month. $8.00 — 12.00.

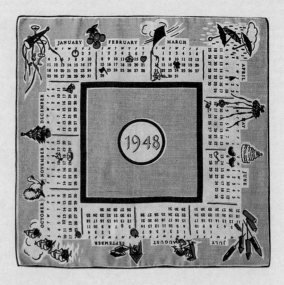

1948 calendar laid out like a game board. $20.00 — 25.00.

1950 is heralded on this calendar. $20.00 — 25.00.

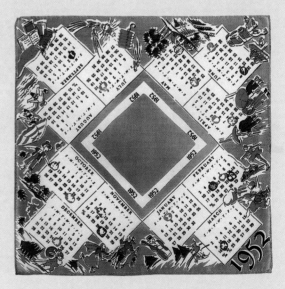

1952 calendar. $10.00 — 15.00.

Where were you in '52? $10.00 — 15.00.

1953, circle the date with holiday motifs. $20.00 — 25.00.

Verbal and visual cues for 1953. $20.00 — 25.00.

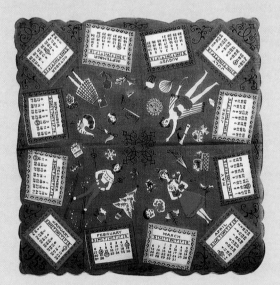

A woman's fashionable approach to 1955. $20.00 — 25.00.

An unusual layout for a 1955 calendar
with borders of four seasons, English and
French (note the crossed sevens). $20.00 — 25.00.

A take off on the popular annual almanacs, in blue. $20.00 — 25.00.

Another take off on the popular annual
almanacs, in gold. $20.00 – 25.00.

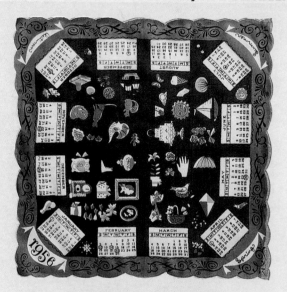

Special occasions are highlighted
in this 1956 hanky. $20.00 – 25.00.

1956 calendar, "She loves me, she loves me not"
daisies, in French. $20.00 – 25.00.

Time flies with this contemporary 1957
calendar, dessin depose. $25.00 – 30.00.

1958 calendar, a year in the life of a woman. $25.00 – 30.00.

1965 Spanish holiday themed
calendar, by Martz. $10.00 – 15.00.

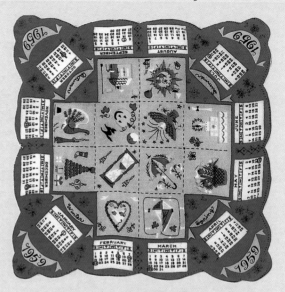

Schematized symbols of the four seasons
on this 1959 calendar. $18.00 – 24.00.

1959 Christmas gift to last the
year round, by Kreier. $12.00 – 15.00.

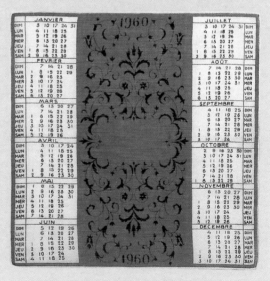

Delicate 1960 calendar with days and
months of the year in French. $20.00 – 25.00.

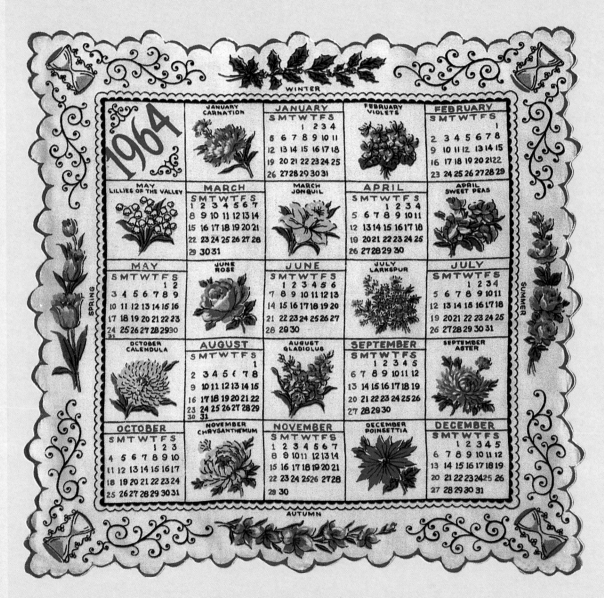

Flowers of the month, 1964. $6.00 — 10.00.

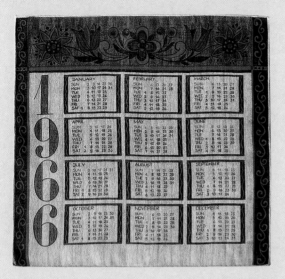

Earth tones on a desk set style
calendar herald 1966. $6.00 — 10.00.

This 1968 circular calendar, floral trim,
could double as a doily. $10.00 — 15.00.

Virgo, the virgin, by Tammis Keefe. $35.00 — 40.00.

Gemini, the twins, by Tammis Keefe. $35.00 — 40.00.

This jewel of a hanky pictures flowers and birthstones for each month. $20.00 — 25.00.

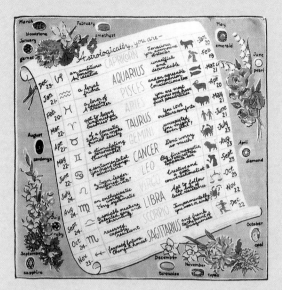

"Astrologically, you are" on a scroll. $10.00 – 15.00.

Tammis Keefe's take on certain signs of the zodiac, "created by Kimball" label. $30.00 – 35.00.

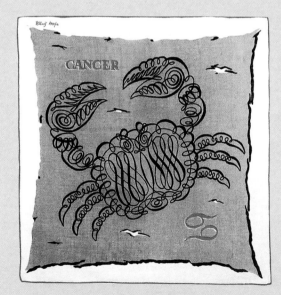

Cancer, the crab, by Tammis Keefe. $35.00 – 40.00.

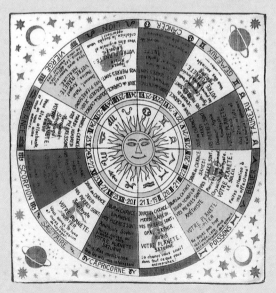

Sun and star signs, in French. $20.00 – 25.00.

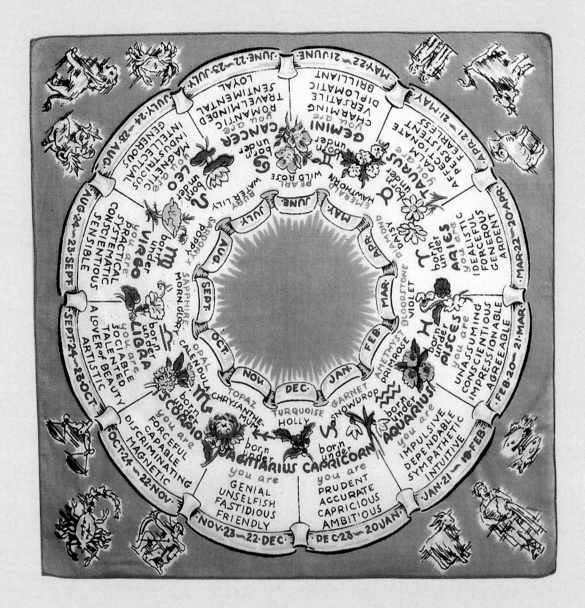

Astrological signs and their characteristics, "a Burmel original" label. $15.00 – 20.00.

Pisces, explaining "his" and "her" attributes, "design registered" bottom right. $10.00 – 15.00.

A similar design in German for Scorpios, explaining "his" and "her" attributes. $10.00 – 15.00.

Aquarius. $25.00 – 30.00.

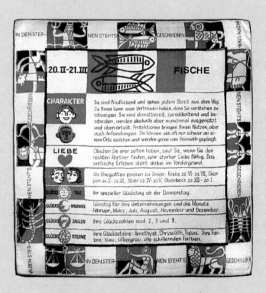

Pisces, German. $30.00 – 35.00.

ADVICE
How to Do Just About Everything

"Advice, n. the smallest current coin."
Ambrose Bierce, *The Devil's Dictionary*

We come from a society where we love to learn, and hankies are an excellent tool. Since their inception, hankies carried a variety of messages for their owner to study. Hankies relayed fairy tales to children and even showed soldiers how to load a gun. It wasn't easy running a house and raising kids, and perhaps even working, so these instructive hankies, often humorous, showed women how to save time.

Kreier's now-quaint view of resolutions
to make a good wife. $30.00 – 40.00.

The Whimsey Report in diagrams. $30.00 – 40.00.

How to keep your husband — ditto,
and in French, too! $45.00 – 55.00.

"How to get the nice things in life," a woman's
wish list to the finer things. $40.00 – 50.00.

How to get a husband — would that it were this easy! $40.00 — 50.00.

Ways to beat insomnia — helpful hints for a good nights sleep, © Franshaw 1954. $50.00 — 60.00.

How to fight insomnia — more tactics for getting to sleep, Kreier. $50.00 — 60.00.

How to give up smoking — a whimsical approach to a serious problem, dessin depose. $50.00 — 60.00.

How to cure a hangover, recipes for the morning after, dessin depose. $45.00 — 55.00.

How to stop snoring (in English and French) — a problem for women the world over. $50.00 – 60.00.

How to ski — the ups and downs of skiing. $40.00 – 50.00.

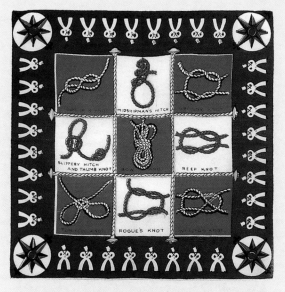

A guide to making sailors' knots. $20.00 – 30.00.

Culbertson's Contact Bridge — a humorous
look at the rules of the game. $40.00 – 50.00.

Culbertson's Key to Canasta — how to
play a favorite card game. $40.00 – 50.00.

Key to your dreams, how to interpret them. $40.00 — 50.00.

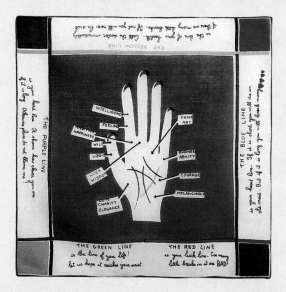

Give yourself a hand and read your future. $60.00 – 70.00.

A visual "Do It Yourself" — don't try these at home. $60.00 – 70.00.

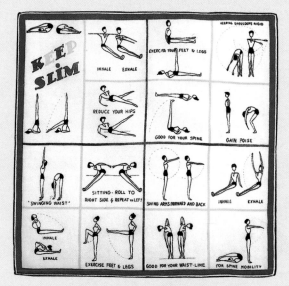

Keep Slim — a reminder that some things never change. $40.00 – 50.00.

How to Keep Cool — sweet drinks to cool you off. $25.00 – 30.00.

Parlez-vous Francais? Bilingual vocabulary guide. $30.00 – 35.00.

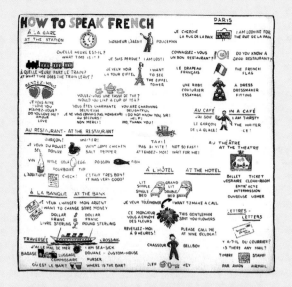

How to speak French, the myth that every cultured woman in America could parler francais. $18.00 – 20.00.

How to Win (in English and French), remember these tips while gambling, dessin depose. $60.00 – 70.00.

How to speak Spanish — feel at home at the bullfights or in Barcelona. $20.00 – 25.00.

How to speak Italian, there's more to Italian than pizza and Pavarotti. $20.00 – 25.00.

TRAVEL
Wish You Were Here!

"I traveled each and ev'ry highway..."
Paul Anka, *My Way*

When the war was over, and gas rationing discontinued, masses of Americans bought their first cars and took to the road for annual vacations. New highways were built, making criss-crossing the country much easier. "See the USA in your Chevrolet" was Dinah Shore's theme song that got a nation up and out.

No city in the world had more energy than New York. Visitors flooded the city every year — to go to Broadway plays, see the sights, and eat in fine restaurants. Ezra Pound said, "New York, the most beautiful city in the world? Here is our poetry, for we have pulled down the stars to our will."

After the war, many servicemen came home from Europe infatuated with everything that was French — wine, bread, architecture, clothing, and even poodles. The French had style and whatever they had or did was better than ours. So we emulated them, began to visit France, and fell under the spell of their culture.

French-themed hankies are plentiful, whereas those with south-of-the-border themes are rare. Strangely, one can find a plethora of tablecloths and salt and pepper shakers but not hankies.

Railroad logos signal a pleasant journey. $30.00 — 40.00.

Bon voyage USA, with 48 states scattered, by Carl Tait. $35.00 — 40.00.

Terrific bouquet of flowers with states around the border. $25.00 — 30.00.

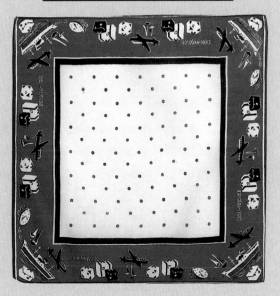

Travel by air and sea for a bon voyage. $10.00 — 15.00.

A bon voyage using images from the early years of air travel. $35.00 — 40.00.

Bon voyage, with "I love you," the universal language, by Kreier. $40.00 — 50.00.

An exuberant bon voyage message, by Carl Tait. $40.00 — 45.00.

A bon voyage hanky from the golden era of travel by sea. $40.00 — 50.00.

A bon voyage, up, up, and away. $5.00 — 10.00.

A safari souvenir, dessin depose. $50.00 — 60.00.

"However you go, have a wonderful trip!," by Panda. $15.00 — 20.00.

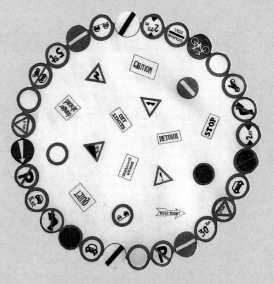

Circle of road signs for drivers at home and abroad. $20.00 — 25.00.

A modern look at classic road signs. $15.00 — 20.00.

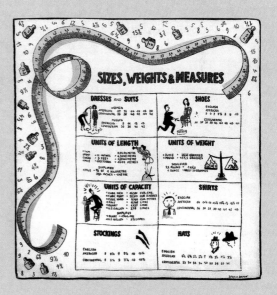

Sizes, weights, and measures. How to shop wherever you are. $40.00 — 50.00.

Hot and cold: gauges temperatures around the world. $40.00 — 50.00.

Universal symbols for road travel,
dessin depose. $40.00 — 50.00.

Bon voyage: helpful hints for
airborne travelers. $40.00 — 50.00.

Reminders of London, by Kreier. $10.00 — 15.00.

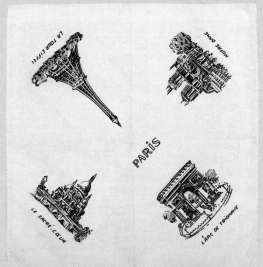

Parisian monuments. $5.00 — 10.00.

COUNTRY:	FOR:	U.S.$	SWISS FRANCS	COUNTRY:	FOR:	U.S.$	SWISS FRANCS
ARGENTINE	100 PESOS	7.29	31.65	ITALY	100 LIRE	-.16	-.70
AUSTRALIA	1 POUND	2.26	9.80	JAPAN	100 YEN	-.28	1.21
AUSTRIA	100 SCHILLING	3.89	16.90	LEBANON	1 POUND	-.26	1.14
BAHAMAS	1 POUND	2.80	12.20	MEXICO	100 PESOS	11.65	50.55
BELGIUM	100 FRANCS	2.02	8.75	NORWAY	100 KRONEN	14.10	61.25
BERMUDA	1 POUND	2.80	12.20	PAKISTAN	100 RUPIEN	30.41	132.-
BRAZIL	100 CRUZEIROS	5.50	23.90	PERU	1 SOL	-.07	-.29
CANADA	1 DOLLAR	1.005	4.37	PORTUGAL	100 ESCUDOS	3.40	14.80
CUBA	1 PESO	1.-	4.34	SOUTH AFRICA	1 POUND	2.80	12.20
DENMARK	100 KRONEN	14.57	63.25	SPAIN	100 PESETAS	2.56	11.10
EGYPT	1 POUND	2.30	10.-	SWEDEN	100 KRONEN	19.47	84.50
FINLAND	100 MARK	-.43	1.87	SWITZERLAND	100 FRANCS	23.05	100.-
FRANCE	100 FRANCS	-.29	1.25	TANGER	100 FRANCS	-.24	1.05
GREAT BRITAIN	1 POUND	2.80	12.20	TURKEY	1 POUND	-.36	1.56
HOLLAND	100 GULDEN	26.52	115.10	U.S.A	1 DOLLAR	1.00	4.30
HONGKONG	1 HONGKONG DOLLAR	-.18	-.76	URUGUAY	1 PESO	-.39	1.70
INDIA	100 RUPIEN	21.20	92.-	VENEZUELA	1 BOLIVAR	-.30	1.31
ISRAEL	1 POUND	1.40	6.08	WESTERN GERMANY	100 D MARK	23.99	104.10

DESSIN DEPOSE

Currency converter, dessin depose. $40.00 — 50.00.

Famous street signs of Paris, by Dewe. $15.00 — 20.00.

United Kingdom handkerchief. $8.00 — 12.00.

Kobenhavn (Copenhagen in Danish), with
letters stitched onto a bag. $15.00 — 20.00.

Montreux in the swinging 1960s. $5.00 — 10.00.

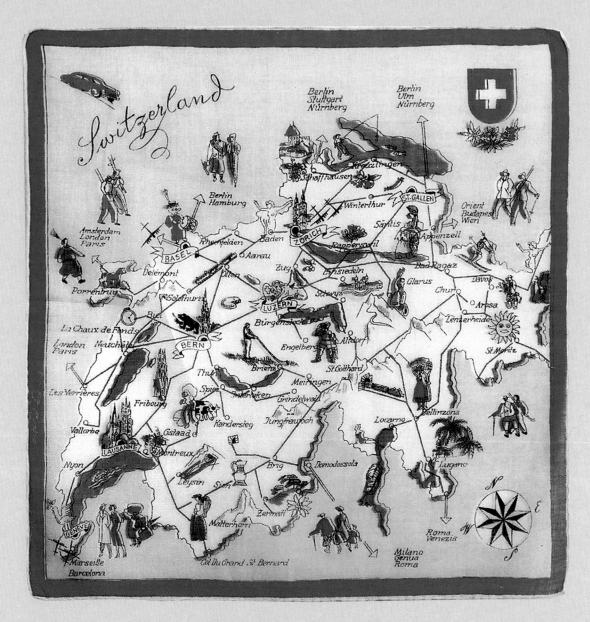

Map of Switzerland. $5.00 — 10.00.

Traveler's guide to London. $15.00 — 20.00.

Traveler's guide to Zurich. $15.00 — 20.00.

Traveler's guide to Canada. $15.00 — 20.00.

An overview of Canada and the
maple leaf emblem. $20.00 — 25.00.

A map of state flowers. $15.00 — 20.00.

A variation with monuments. $15.00 — 20.00.

Mexico with many cities and sights noted. $15.00 — 20.00.

Asia at a glance. $15.00 — 20.00.

Puerto Rico for tourists. $15.00 — 20.00.

Traveler's guide to New York City. $30.00 — 40.00.

Colonial highlights of New England. $15.00 – 20.00.

Sites of New England. $20.00 – 25.00.

More sites of New England. $15.00 – 20.00.

Long Island, New York. $20.00 – 25.00.

Traveler's guide to New Jersey. $20.00 — 25.00.

Florida hibiscus. $10.00 – 15.00.

Connecticut living, by Carl Tait. $35.00 – 40.00.

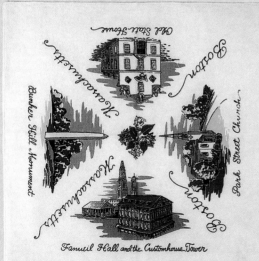

Historic sites in Boston. $10.00 – 15.00.

Petticoat Lane, Kansas City. $10.00 – 15.00.

Yours 'til Niagara Falls. $10.00 — 15.00.

Souvenir of the Seattle World's Fair. $20.00 — 25.00.

Let freedom ring — Philadelphia — with words from the Constitution. $10.00 — 15.00.

Franklin Parkway, Philadelphia, by Tammis Keefe. $30.00 — 35.00.

Meet me at the Eagle, Philadelphia — a meeting place for visitors in Center City, by Tammis Keefe. $15.00 — 20.00.

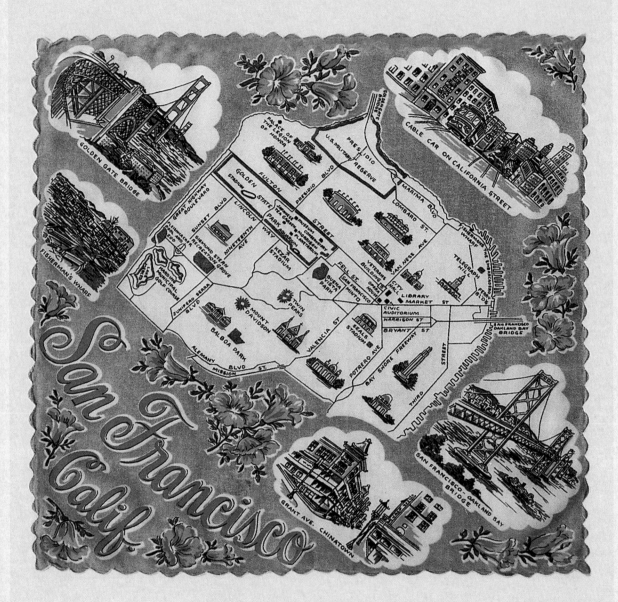

Melange of San Francisco sights. $15.00 — 20.00.

A visual pun — a circular view "around" San Francisco. $12.00 — 15.00.

Los Angeles sights. $15.00 — 20.00.

Wilmington, Delaware, by Tammis Keefe. $30.00 — 35.00.

Olvera Street, a bit of old Mexico in Los Angeles. $5.00 — 10.00.

Our nation's capital, Washington, DC. $10.00 — 15.00.

Olvera St., Los Angeles, by Tammis Keefe. $40.00 – 45.00.

Visual pun "around" Cleveland. $8.00 – 10.00.

Sites to see in Denver, the Mile High City. $10.00 – 15.00.

Tinseltown, a Hollywood premiere,
by Tammis Keefe. $35.00 – 40.00.

Way down yonder in New Orleans, by Carl Tait. $40.00 — 45.00.

Wrigley Building, Chicago, by Tammis Keefe. $40.00 – 45.00.

Hartford, the home of insurance. $5.00 – 10.00.

Sturbridge Village. $6.00 – 8.00.

Laguna Beach, California, by Tammis Keefe. $40.00 – 45.00.

Souvenir menu from Swissair. $5.00 — 10.00.

Lady Liberty, by Tammis Keefe. $45.00 — 50.00.

Central Park Zoo, by Tammis Keefe. $45.00 — 50.00.

Times Square, by Tammis Keefe. $45.00 — 50.00.

Park Avenue, by Tammis Keefe. $45.00 — 50.00.

Greenwich Village's Washington Square, by Tammis Keefe. $45.00 — 50.00.

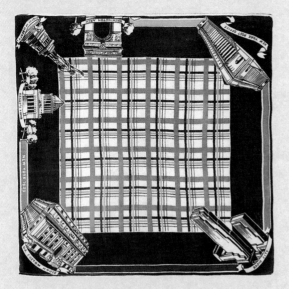

New York monuments — where's the
Empire State Building? $40.00 – 45.00.

Aerial view of the 1939
New York World's Fair. $50.00 – 60.00.

Well-known sites of the big city, including the Trylon
and Perisphere of the 1939 World's Fair. $40.00 – 50.00.

Exhibition halls of the 1939
New York World's Fair. $30.00 – 35.00.

Unisphere and other sites of New York commemorating the 1964 World's Fair. $20.00 — 25.00.

Columbus Circle, New York, by Tammis Keefe. $40.00 — 45.00.

New York World's Fair, Swiss Air/Switzerland
Pavilion 1964 — 1965, after original mosaics
by F. Petermann, Lausanne, Switzerland. $20.00 — 25.00.

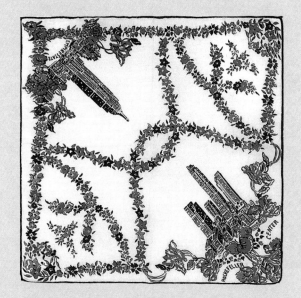

Rockefeller Center and Empire State. $10.00 — 15.00.

Postcard views of New York. $5.00 — 10.00.

Unusual lower Manhattan and Brooklyn sites, including the
Brooklyn Bridge and Ebbetts Field, by Tammis Keefe. $40.00 — 45.00.

New York skyline. $20.00 – 25.00.

Around New York City, on round floral
hanky — a visual pun. $8.00 – 12.00.

Some of the finest the city had
to offer in 1939. $20.00 – 25.00.

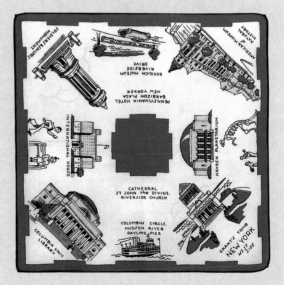

Places to see and things to do. $30.00 – 35.00.

The United Nations surrounded by trompe l'oeil postcards from countries around the world. $15.00 — 20.00.

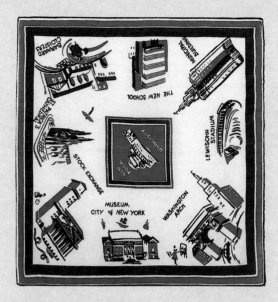

New York University and its environs. $20.00 – 25.00.

Atlas and Radio City. $25.00 – 30.00.

A Dwaine Meek collage of New York
views, paper Kimball label. $8.00 – 12.00.

Another Dwaine Meek collage of
New York views. $8.00 – 12.00.

Carl Tait's view of bustling New York. $35.00 — 45.00.

Key monuments in New York, done
in Art Deco manner. $15.00 — 20.00.

Streamline monuments of New York. $20.00 — 25.00.

Diagram of aerial view of New
York City. $15.00 — 20.00.

Fabulous eye-popping New York skyline. $40.00 — 50.00.

A rear window of lively Paris. $15.00 — 20.00.

Try this beauty regime (in French). $30.00 — 40.00.

To the rescue, by Frederique. $10.00 — 15.00.

Mysterious correspondence to a mysterious mademoiselle Paris/New York, French and English. $15.00 — 20.00.

Pour vous Madame (for you Madame) — a mystery missive. $15.00 — 20.00.

Le Printemps a Paris (springtime in Paris), by Francoise Durieux. $10.00 — 15.00.

Demure coquette at the Eiffel Tower. $8.00 — 12.00.

An artist's studio, Vie de Boheme (Bohemian life), by Francoise Durieux, paper label, Glamour Girl. $10.00 — 15.00.

A lively and full day at the Tuileries Garden. $10.00 — 15.00.

The flower market at the Madelaine with morphed poodles, by Jean Hanai. $10.00 — 15.00.

Doggy at the Place Pigalle, by Jean Hanai. $10.00 — 15.00.

All the things a Spanish dancer needs,
by Mary Lewis. $10.00 — 15.00.

Abstract pattern comprised of Mexican
pottery and sombreros. $15.00 — 20.00.

The liveliness of Mexican music expressed
in the rhythm of placement. $15.00 — 20.00.

Man on burrow, the main transportation used
in the mountains even today. $15.00 — 20.00.

THE FIFTY STATES

From Sea to Shining Sea

These souvenirs become popular after World War II when gas rationing stopped and the general public started taking car trips. State hankies were the ideal souvenirs to bring back to friends and loved ones because they were inexpensive and took up very little room in your car or suitcase. Not only did they make great souvenirs, but they could be used as a guide and road map along the way. And when the drive got boring, you could memorize the capitals and sights of each state.

Alabama. $18.00 – 25.00.

Alaska. $18.00 – 25.00.

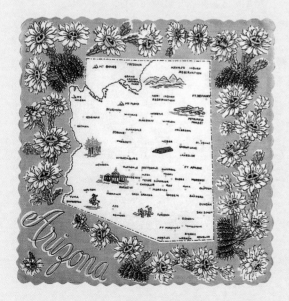

Arizona. $18.00 – 25.00.

Arkansas. $18.00 – 25.00.

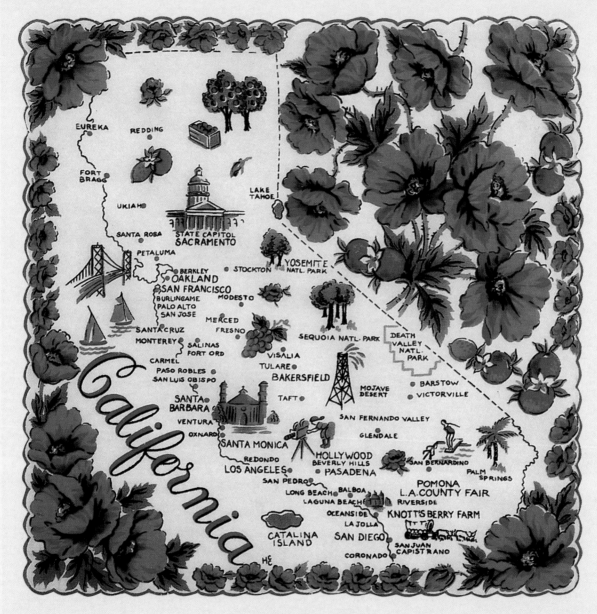

California. $18.00 — 25.00.

Colorado. $18.00 — 25.00.

Connecticut. $15.00 — 18.00.

Delaware. $15.00 — 18.00.

Florida. $20.00 — 25.00.

Georgia. $18.00 — 25.00.

Hawaii. $20.00 — 25.00.

Idaho. $18.00 — 25.00.

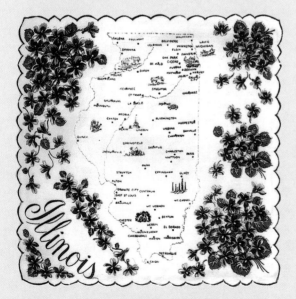

Illinois. $18.00 — 25.00.

Indiana. $18.00 — 25.00.

Iowa. $18.00 — 25.00.

Kansas. $18.00 — 25.00.

Kentucky. $18.00 — 25.00.

Louisiana. $18.00 — 25.00.

Maine. $18.00 — 25.00.

Maryland. $18.00 — 25.00.

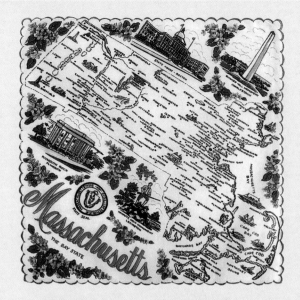

Massachusetts. $18.00 – 25.00.

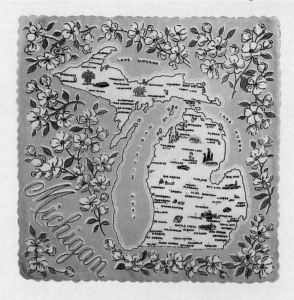

Michigan. $18.00 – 25.00.

Minnesota. $18.00 – 25.00.

Mississippi. $18.00 – 25.00.

Missouri. $18.00 — 25.00.

Montana. $18.00 — 25.00.

Nebraska. $18.00 — 25.00.

Nevada. $18.00 — 25.00.

New Hampshire. $18.00 — 25.00.

New Jersey. $18.00 — 25.00.

New Mexico. $18.00 — 25.00.

New York. $18.00 — 25.00.

North Carolina. $18.00 — 25.00.

North Dakota. $18.00 — 25.00.

Ohio. $18.00 — 25.00.

Oklahoma. $18.00 — 25.00.

Oregon. $18.00 — 25.00.

Pennsylvania. $20.00 — 25.00.

Rhode Island. $18.00 — 25.00.

South Carolina. $18.00 – 25.00.

South Dakota. $18.00 — 25.00.

Tennessee. $18.00 — 25.00.

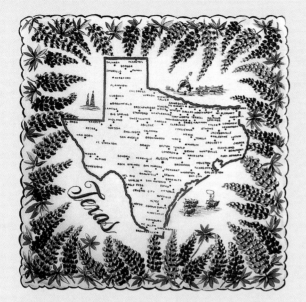

Texas. $18.00 — 25.00.

Utah. $18.00 — 25.00.

Vermont. $18.00 — 25.00.

Virginia. $18.00 — 25.00.

Washington. $18.00 – 25.00.

West Virginia. $18.00 — 25.00.

Wisconsin. $18.00 — 25.00.

Wyoming. $18.00 — 25.00.

Jigsaw look at the 48 states. $10.00 — 15.00.

HISTORY & POLITICS
Colorful Commemoratives

"Politics is still the greatest and the most honorable adventure."
John Buchan, Lord Tweedsmuir, *Pilgrim's Way*

In the past, hankies were often printed with political and history lessons like letters to be looked at and passed along. These political messages were worn like campaign buttons, useful in "getting the message out." Can you think of a better way to memorize the Declaration of Independance, the succession of Presidents, or the great innovations?

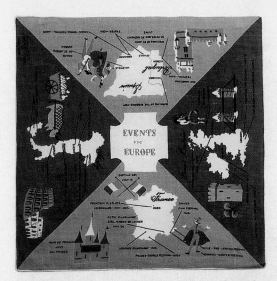

Plan your next trip to Europe around these festivals and events, May 1956, by Tammis O'Keefe (unusual to have a dated hanky). $30.00 – 40.00.

Technological firsts — pre-computer. $15.00 – 20.00.

Formative events in our nation's early history — good for preparing for Jeopardy! $10.00 – 15.00.

Feminine red, white, and blue flowers in honor of the seamstress of the first American Flag. $10.00 – 15.00.

Let Freedom Ring, the Liberty Bell, by Tammis Keefe. $30.00 – 40.00.

Where it all began — Independence Hall
in Philadelphia, by Tammis Keefe. $30.00 – 40.00.

We the people, City of Brotherly Love,
Philadelphia, by Tammis Keefe. $30.00 – 40.00.

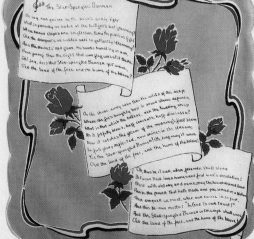

The lyrics of the Star Spangled
Banner, including the second and third
stanzas — seldom sung. $20.00 – 25.00.

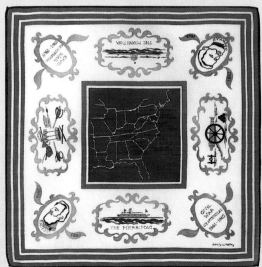

Hundredth anniversary of the Civil War, including
famous battle sites, signed Emily Whaley. $10.00 – 15.00.

Recognizable World War II victory sign in patriotic colors. $10.00 – 15.00.

US Navy wives' hankies. $10.00 — 15.00.

Chart of presidents and years in office up to Dwight D. Eisenhower, think of everyone who's missing, © Franshaw 1954. $25.00 — 30.00.

History of the Democratic party and presidents through Harry S. Truman. $25.00 — 30.00.

History of the GOP through Eisenhower. $25.00 — 30.00.

Yet another designer, Jeanne Miller, depicts Democratic donkeys celebrating a victory at the polls. This hanky comes in at least two other colors, gray and gold. $25.00 — 30.00.

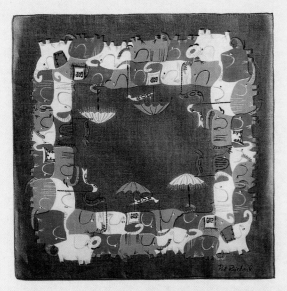

A stampede of Republican elephants. $20.00 – 25.00.

Babar-like Republican elephants urge you to vote, fringed blue hanky. $8.00 – 12.00.

Elephants dream of GOP victories from coast to coast. $20.00 – 25.00.

This one did the trick, Eisenhower was elected for two terms. $40.00 – 50.00.

ABSTRACTIONS
The Pattern's the Thing

The industrial age, with its advances in science and inventions from cars to rockets, brought about new designs in furniture and fabrics. Artists, like Calder and Miro, were in the forefront, including in their works elements related to the machine age, as well as newly discussed symbols. It was natural for hanky designers, artists in their own right, to incorporate some of these ideas when creating hankies.

Flamboyant ribbon and polka dots. $15.00 — 20.00.

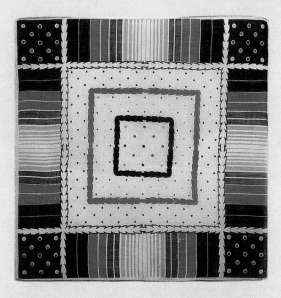

Rhythmic assortment of stripes and spots. $8.00 — 12.00.

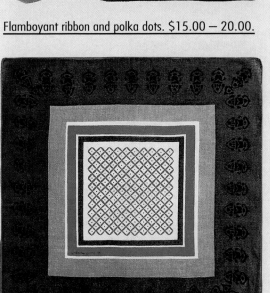

Sophisticated concentric squares,
by Emily Whaley. $15.00 — 20.00.

Woven design gives texture to the hanky. $15.00 — 20.00.

Squares within squares demarcated by a twisted rope pattern. $15.00 — 20.00.

Pretty in pink — sherbet rectangles surrounding a pink square. $15.00 — 20.00.

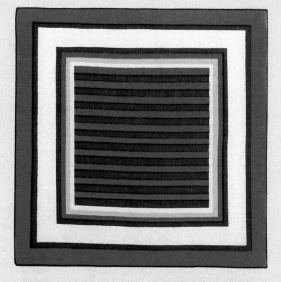

Optical design in primary colors. $15.00 — 20.00.

Maze in bold colors. $15.00 — 20.00.

Primitive images off-center on an olive ground, signed Wilcke. $15.00 — 20.00.

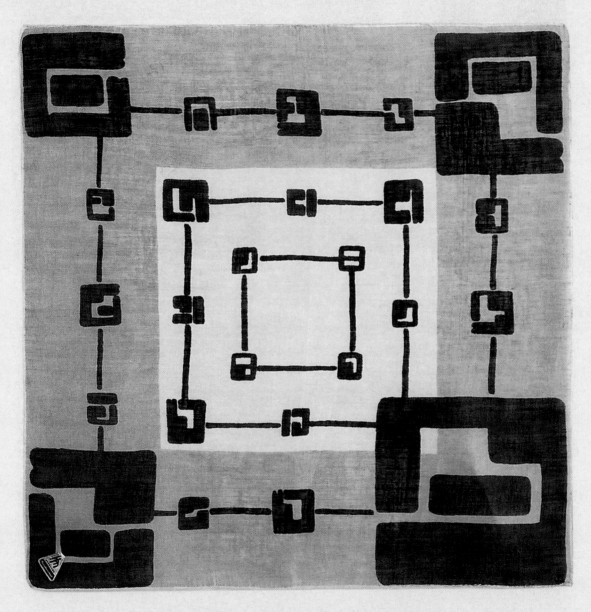

Shades of gray, paper label, Herrmann. $15.00 — 20.00.

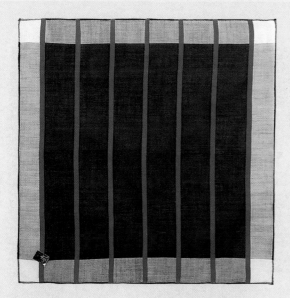

With hints of Amish design, paper label. $15.00 — 20.00.

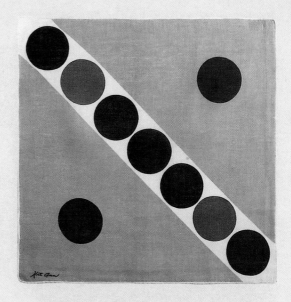

Blue on blue, by Kit Ann. $15.00 — 20.00.

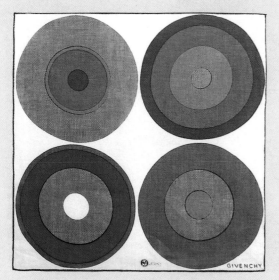

A visual brain teaser, four varying concentric circles.
Are any alike? Stamped Givenchy, Bloch Freres,
all linen, hand rolled. $15.00 — 20.00.

Deep orange geometric design,
stamped Givenchy. $15.00 — 20.00.

211

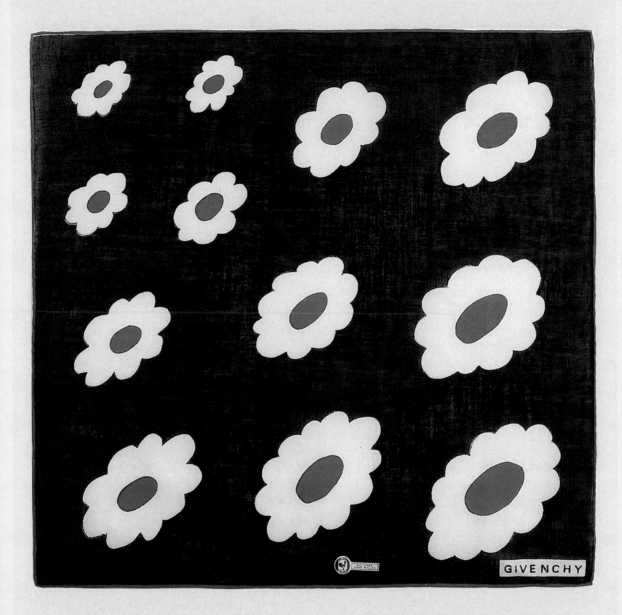

Abstracted daisies with pink centers, Givenchy, Bloch Freres, all linen, hand rolled. $15.00 — 20.00.

Givenchy sets sail in orange and white. $15.00 — 20.00.

An abstract design conveying the feeling
of a collage, by Givenchy. $15.00 — 20.00.

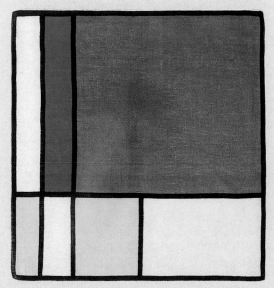

To go with your Mondrian dress! $15.00 — 20.00.

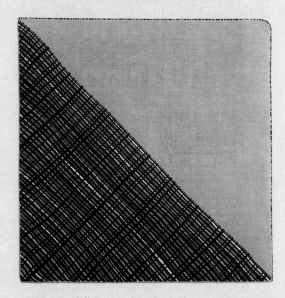

An optical illusion makes this look woven. Note
the colorful edges on the solid side. $8.00 — 12.00.

Scottish tartan plaid. $4.00 — 8.00.

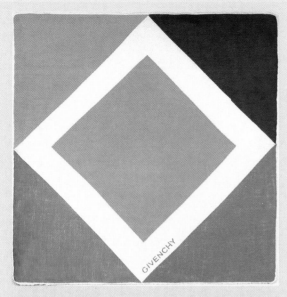

Square on point, stamped Givenchy. $15.00 — 20.00.

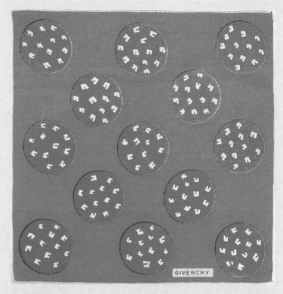

Repeating circles, stamped Givenchy. $15.00 — 20.00.

Another plaid. $4.00 — 8.00.

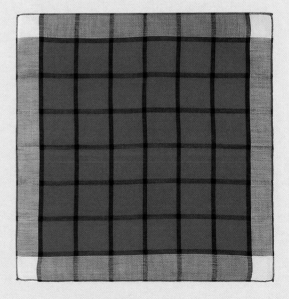

A red plaid hanky. $4.00 — 8.00.

FASHION
What the Well-Dressed Woman Wears

"Old fashions please me best."
William Shakespeare, *Taming of the Shrew*, Act III, Scene I

Women either carried hankies in their purses or wore them like corsages, cascading out of jacket or blouse breast pockets. Women chose their hankies every day to match their outfit and/or their mood. That the subjects of some hankies were comments on fashion is natural and amusing. After all, shopping and style were of endless interest to most women.

Hints on dressing for different body types. $20.00 — 30.00.

Gay nineties dressmaker's model
and patterns, by Kati. $12.00 — 16.00.

What the well-dressed Victorian woman
wears as the weather changes. $15.00 — 20.00.

Umbrellas, signed Faith Austin. $20.00 — 25.00.

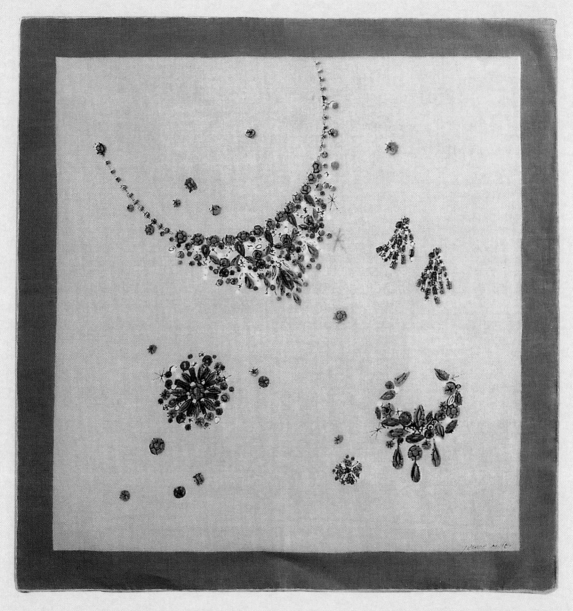

Jewels, by Jeanne Miller —— a parure, but where's the tiara? $10.00 – 15.00.

Hats and hat boxes, by Faith Austin,
paper label by Kimball. $20.00 — 25.00.

Chic shoes, by Kati. $20.00 — 25.00.

Gloves for day and evening, by Kati. $20.00 — 25.00.

A wardrobe happily drying in the sun,
dessin depose. $25.00 — 30.00.

A window filled with hairstyles, by Pat Prichard. $25.00 — 30.00.

Hats and more hats, signed Bonheur. $8.00 — 12.00.

Hats and hat pins, by Erin O'Dell. $8.00 — 12.00.

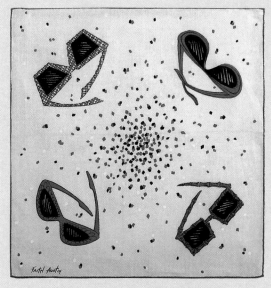

Stylish shades. $30.00 — 35.00.

Apres ski — take it all off! Dessin depose. $15.00 — 20.00.

Tools of the trade, by hat designer Sally Victor. $10.00 — 15.00.

Accessories for a cultural evening
out, by Ceil Chapman. $10.00 — 15.00.

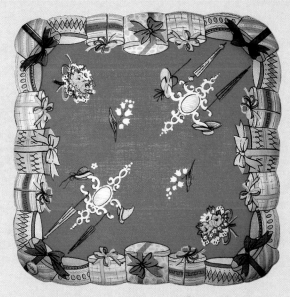

Hatboxes form a vivid border. $15.00 — 20.00.

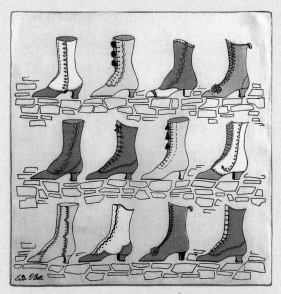

High-button shoes, by Erin O'Dell. $20.00 — 25.00.

Carl Tait's message for a rainy day. $40.00 — 45.00.

Girls on the go, by Kreier. $10.00 — 15.00.

Silhouettes as seen through
a beach umbrella. $30.00 – 40.00.

Jeanne Miller's assortment of
perfume bottles. $8.00 – 12.00.

Jeanne Miller's something for a rainy day. $8.00 – 12.00.

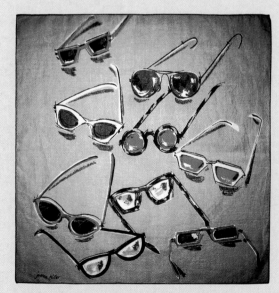

Jeanne Miller's collection of sunglasses. $15.00 – 20.00.

BOTANICAL
Florals & Forest

"And be sure to smell the flowers along the way."

Walter Hagen, *The Walter Hagen Story*

"When you take a flower in your hand and really look at it,
it's your world for the moment."

Georgia O'Keeffe

Hankies depicting flowers and leaves are the most common, least expensive of all vintage hankies. Most women love flowers because they're cheerful and feminine. It's no surprise that flowered hankies became the perfect gift for your child's teacher or husband's aunt, especially when you didn't want to spend a lot or didn't know the woman's size or taste. Every woman could always use a fresh hanky! Since the hanky industry originated on the east coast, most of the floral and woodland subjects are drawn from standard east coast gardens and countryside. It's amazing how realistic these flowers and leaves can be and how a season can be conjured up by a few abstract dashes of color. These hankies provided the wearer with the opportunity, for very little, to reflect the new season.

A group shot of flowers.

A group shot of
seasonal flowers.

A curved element behind emphasizes
the stylized hibiscus. $5.00 — 7.00.

Brambles, leather fern, and a collection
of fall leaves, paper label. $15.00 — 18.00.

Lotus flowers and fern reflecting eastern spring woodland scene. $10.00 — 15.00.

Butterfly and peony blossom. $5.00 — 7.00.

Red roses with scalloped edges (Did you know that there are people who only collect scalloped hankies?). $4.00 — 6.00.

A potpourri of flower pots. $3.00 — 5.00.

Chrysanthemums and asters, paper label Burmel. $6.00 — 8.00.

229

Giant red anemones. $4.00 — 6.00.

Perimeter rows of yellow roses with baby's breath. $3.00 — 5.00.

Multicolored poppies. $3.00 — 5.00.

An abstracted bouquet of forget-me-nots
in bright colors. $3.00 — 5.00.

Pansies. $10.00 — 15.00.

Dogwood, a favorite fifties tree, the emblem of spring. $4.00 — 6.00.

Roses against a trompe l'oeil
background, by Billy Kompa. $3.00 — 5.00.

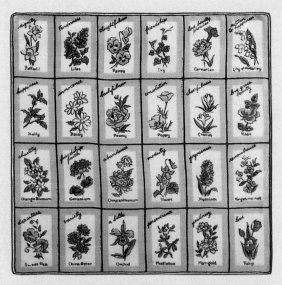

Flowers and their human attributes. $3.00 — 5.00.

Flowers identified with months of the year. $8.00 — 12.00.

Sprigs of herbs. $8.00 — 12.00.

The goings-on at a flower market. $10.00 — 15.00.

Romance at the flower market. $10.00 — 15.00.

Bold daffodils. $3.00 — 5.00.

Sprouting daffodils, paper label. $3.00 — 5.00.

Tiger lilies on scalloped field. $3.00 — 5.00.

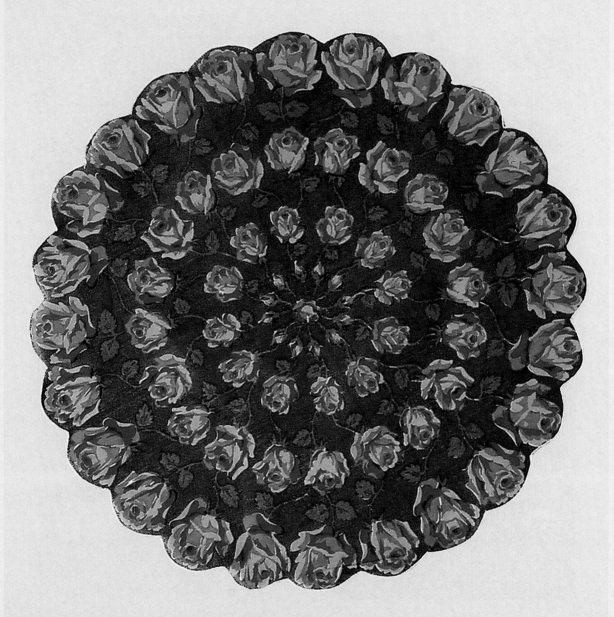

Concentric circles of roses. $6.00 — 8.00.

Unique giant blue poppy with scrolling element, asymmetrically scalloped. $3.00 — 5.00.

Nosegays of violets. $4.00 — 6.00.

Concentric petals in a three-dimensional pattern. $3.00 — 5.00.

Purple pansies against a candy cane field. $3.00 — 5.00.

Red tulips, scalloped edges. $4.00 — 6.00.

Giant purple mum scalloped to follow
shape of the petals. $15.00 — 20.00.

Pink hibiscus flowers scalloped to fit petals. $15.00 — 20.00.

Zinnias outlined by acid green ground,
by Monique, paper label. $3.00 — 5.00.

Charming multicolored bouquet of poppies, daisies, and fox-
glove on latticed chocolate brown ground. $8.00 — 12.00.

Chrysanthemums bursting through leaves. $6.00 – 8.00.

Pink horse chestnut leaf in mirror image. $6.00 — 8.00.

Blue chestnut leaf hanky, paper sticker, Carol Stanley. $6.00 — 8.00.

Maple, alder, oak, and poplar in rich autumn colors, by Thomas Fisher. $4.00.

Maple leaves and seeds in rust and blue, by Faith Austin. $15.00 — 20.00.

Autumn oak leaves, by Faith Austin. $10.00 – 15.00.

Boston ivy in classic autumn colors. $6.00 — 8.00.

Painterly approach to deciduous trees,
some with leaves, some without. $6.00 — 8.00.

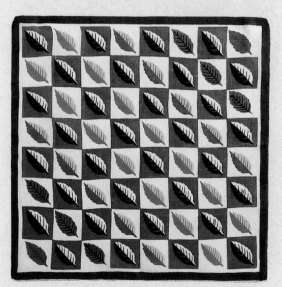

Cookie cutter optical elm leaves. $12.00 — 15.00.

An array of Boston ivy. $6.00 — 8.00.

Solomon's seal with flowers. $8.00 — 12.00.

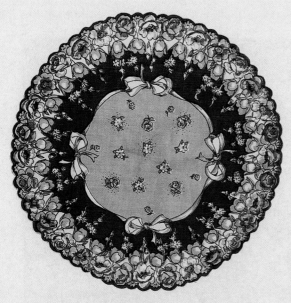

Circular floral motifs with bows. $4.00 — 8.00.

Roses on branch. $4.00 — 8.00.

A single spectacular orchid. $12.00 — 15.00.

Stylized tulips, by Jean D'Orly , Paris. $12.00 — 15.00.

Autumn leaves. $10.00 — 15.00.

Sophisticated color combination. $3.00 — 8.00.

Pansies. $8.00 — 10.00.

Bright autumn combination. $4.00 — 8.00.

Deep borders of fantasy roses. $3.00 — 8.00.

Majestic maple leaves. $10.00 — 15.00.

Charming pansy circle. $10.00 — 15.00.

An arrangement of leaves. $8.00 — 10.00.

Roses by the dozen. $12.00 — 15.00.

Silkscreen and printed in gold adds
another dimension. $4.00 — 8.00.

CHILDREN
For Our Youngsters

"Age does not make us childish, as they say.
It only finds us true children still."
Johann Wolfgang von Goethe, *Faust.* The First Part. Prelude on the Stage

Handkerchiefs, smaller than those made for adults, were manufactured for children. Carrying a hanky like Mommy and Daddy made little ones feel very grown-up. Hanky designers lost no time in providing children with nursery rhymes and parables. Fairy tales, proverbs, and comics, many popularized by Disney, taught lessons of happiness and love, even closure. With the advent of TV, the proliferation of movie theaters, and the development of animation, sources of inspiration for hanky artists rapidly grew.

Watch out Mr. Penguin!, by Tom Lamb. $22.00 — 28.00.

Funny elephant dancing to a mouse quartet, by Tom Lamb. $22.00 — 28.00.

Scottie lass in blue, by Tom Lamb. $22.00 — 28.00.

Cockers always hit a homerun. $8.00 — 10.00.

Howdy on bucking bronco, © Bob Smith. Bringing cowboys and the west into our lives was an attempt to bring us back to a gentler time after the war. It worked for a while, as Howdy Doody was the most popular TV program from 1947 until about 1960. At the start of each show, Buffalo Bob would ask the kids in the peanut gallery, "Hey kids, what time is it?" and they'd enthusiastically call out "It's Howdy Doody Time." $40.00 — 50.00.

Smokey Bear, popular character designed in the 1940s, offers tips to prevent forest fires, by Tom Lamb. $30.00 — 40.00.

It's Howdy Doody Time, © Bob Smith. $40.00 — 50.00.

An elephant farmer and his friends. $5.00 — 10.00.

Dalmatian and piglet sharing a bottle, by Tom Lamb. $22.00 — 28.00.

Mickey, Donald, and Pluto shoot for the stars, © Walt Disney Productions. $30.00 – 40.00.

Mickey Mouse scores a goal, © Walt Disney Productions. $30.00 — 40.00.

Too late, Donald Duck!, © Walt Disney Productions. $25.00 — 35.00.

Shoot 'em up, Disney style, © Walt Disney Productions. $20.00 — 30.00.

Minnie bakes a pie with the help of Jiminy Cricket © Walt Disney Productions. $30.00 — 40.00.

Pajama party, paper label. $6.00 — 8.00.

Old Mother Goose makes the rounds. $8.00 — 10.00.

Willie goat rhyme. $12.00 — 15.00.

Bunny serenading a canary. $12.00 — 15.00.

Baby lion toreador. $12.00 — 15.00.

Giraffes and donkeys munching patterns off the background, signed. $12.00 — 15.00.

Baby lamb on point. $12.00 — 15.00.

Circus hankies in original box. $8.00 — 12.00.

A set of embroidered nursery rhyme
hankies in their original box. $8.00 — 12.00.

Santa delivers. $12.00 — 15.00.

Dionne quintuplets — a wonder of the world. The girls were born in 1934 in Canada, the first quints to survive infancy. They were moved to Quintland and put on view, behind glass for several hours a day, for millions of people to see. By Tom Lamb. $60.00 — 70.00.

Dionne quintuplets — Yvonne, Annette, Cecile, Marie, and Emilie, by Tom Lamb. $60.00 — 70.00.

French miss walking her poodle. $8.00 — 10.00.

Old Mother Goose, a Golden Book design by the Provensens, © S&S. $12.00 — 15.00.

The little kittens and their lost mittens. $10.00 — 15.00.

The Bumsteads of the funny paper fame. $30.00 — 40.00.

Humpty Dumpty's travails. $20.00 — 25.00.

"The porridge is just right!," the three bears. $12.00 — 15.00.

Snow White. $12.00 — 15.00.

Bessie Brooks and Tommy Snooks. $15.00 — 20.00.

The Hare and the Tortoise, by Tom Lamb, one of a series made in the 1930s. $30.00 — 40.00.

The Hanky House book, with the days of the week hankies.
"You're visiting the Hankys, the doors are open wide, the Hanky girls are waiting, so why not go inside.
The Hanky House looks pretty with hanky curtains there, one hanky is for Monday and one for Tuesday's wear.
Hilda plays with Fido each Wednesday 'tis said, she wears her hanky apron, now you'll wear it instead.
The girls eat in the garden at a hanky table too, that hanky is for Thursday and it's nice and fresh and new.
The girls know you like hankies, and washed these right away, so you can wear one Friday and one on Saturday.
And now they're playing Indian; the hanky tent is strong, the best hanky's for Sunday, hope you wear it all day long.
Now you've seen the Hanky house; the birdie sings this tune, "The children like you very much and hope you'll come back soon!"
<u>$50.00 — 75.00.</u>

The Three Bears. $10.00 – 15.00.

Carousel kiddies. $12.00 — 15.00.

Chick and company make learning the ABCs fun.
$10.00 — 15.00.

Boy piping a tune with bluebird
accompanying him. $8.00 — 12.00.

Funny bunnies. $10.00 — 12.00.

By train, plane, or boat. $4.00 – 6.00.

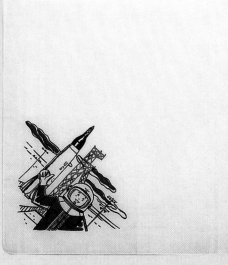

Kid astronaut. $25.00 – 30.00.

Man on the moon. $40.00 – 45.00.

Playful kitties. $12.00 – 15.00.

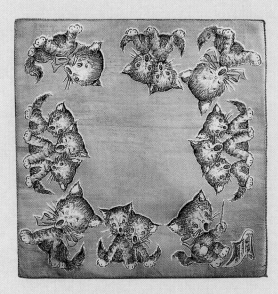

Musical kittens. $4.00 – 6.00.

Rhyme about Nanook, an Eskimo boy. $12.00 — 15.00.

Bucking broncos at the rodeo — children's fantasies of a gentler time came to them through the TV. $15.00 – 20.00.

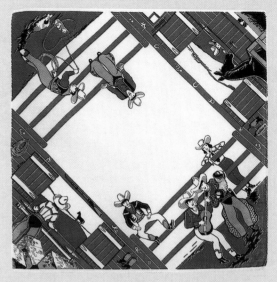

Cowpokes at the corral. $15.00 – 20.00.

A teenager's hanky with girls engrossed in phone calls. $10.00 – 15.00.

Teenage girls strike a pose. $6.00 – 8.00.

Ballerinas on point. $10.00 — 15.00.

Be prepared! $15.00 — 20.00.

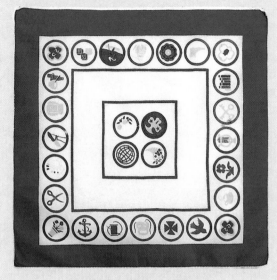

Girl Scouts. $15.00 — 20.00.

Girl Scouts. $10.00 — 15.00.

Brownies. $15.00 — 20.00.

MUSIC
Making Beautiful Melodies

"If music be the food of love, play on."
William Shakespeare, *Twelfth Night,* Act I, Scene I

Music, available through the radio, phonographs, TV, and films, became the subject of hankies — whether as a serious concerto, the jitterbug, or the vinyl records themselves.

Barbershop quartet, special songs,
by Carl Tait. $40.00 — 45.00.

A Carl Tait tour of the sidewalks
of New York. $40.00 — 45.00.

All the words to the Christmas time
classic, by Tammis Keefe. $30.00 — 35.00.

Tammis Keefe's rhythmic
gallery of instruments. $30.00 — 35.00.

Tammis Keefe's scores and instruments. $30.00 — 35.00.

Romance comes with a few
bars of Beethoven. $8.00 – 12.00.

Prom night balloon bliss. $25.00 – 30.00.

Jitterbug on a disc. $25.00 – 30.00.

Fred and Ginger do the piccolino
from Top Hat. $45.00 – 55.00.

ADVERTISEMENTS
Buy Yours Today!

Giveaways and promotions made the public aware of the product.

Amsco's covered wagon toy chest for every young cowboy's and cowgirl's fantasy. $20.00 — 30.00.

A lithe dancer is like a great race horse when it comes to Arthur Murray's Dancers Derby, by Tammis Keefe. $35.00 — 45.00.

What the well-dressed Neiman Marcus cowboy will wear. $25.00 — 35.00.

Repeated Neiman Marcus logo translates into an endless design. $3.00 — 6.00.

Fragrances by Guerlain, famed Paris parfumeur. $4.00 — 8.00.

"For You," shopping on Rue St. Honore. $8.00 — 12.00.

Try this ten-day plan and perhaps you'll be able to wear Vogue fashions. $25.00 — 35.00.

If ten days is too much, try Harper's nine-day Wonder Diet. $25.00 — 35.00.

Take to the road with an XKE. $6.00 — 10.00.

LIPSTICK HANKIES
Ladies, Mind Your Manners

With fire engine red lipstick popular, hostesses worried that women guests would wipe their lips with, and ruin, white dinner napkins or guest towels in the powder room. Red "lipstick hankies" were placed near the sink in bathrooms and on women's plates at dinner parties for women to wipe their lips on before using a napkin.

Lipstick in script with flowers. $2.00 — 4.00.

Shy Southern belle. $2.00 — 4.00.

Embroidered cigarette between parted lips. $2.00 — 4.00.

Ever-popular Scottie, embroidered on red hanky. $2.00 — 4.00.

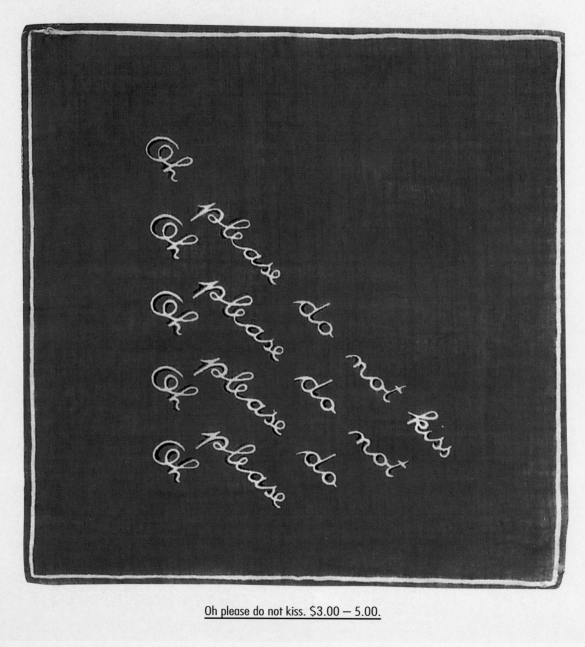

Oh please do not kiss. $3.00 — 5.00.

Pour Le Rouge says it simply. $2.00 — 4.00.

Bordered Pour Le Rouge. $4.00 — 6.00.

Fast women, fast cars, Scandia label, 1963. $10.00 — 15.00.

Too chic! $10.00 — 15.00.

CARE & DECORATIVE USE
Protecting Your Investment

Under ideal conditions, hankies should be treated like other antique textiles. They should be kept flat, wrapped in acid-free paper in a dark place away from sunlight. For the moment, we keep ours in pizza boxes, lined with acid-free paper, but we've ordered photography storage bins. (By the way, Bert says that his favorite of all of Barbara's collections is her hanky collection because it fits under the bed where he doesn't have to look at it!) Often, if you find a hanky in a second-hand shop or a flea market, it will have grime along the fold lines and look "gray." A bath in cool water with mild soap or Woolite may help, but try not to wash it unless you must. Use a cool iron for pressing.

The cost of a hanky varies depending on several factors, including rarity and condition. If it has pin holes or discoloration, no matter how minor, it's worth less than the same hanky in pristine condition. But, if it's a rare example, and you never know when you'll find a better one, you'll want to buy it anyway! Prices vary across the country as well (New York and west coast prices tend to be higher). Therefore, the prices we give provide only a general range. Country auctions, house and garage sales, and online auctions are good sources for inexpensive examples. Be careful with the latter, as you can't see the hankies in the flesh, you must read the descriptions carefully. Sometimes you can get what you want in online auctions for a song, and other times, you might pay more than you would have in an expensive antique shop.

You can use hankies to decorate a room in many ways. You can keep them in scrapbooks on your coffee table for guests to leaf through and enjoy. You can make quilts and pillows for your beds or sofas. You can even make clothes with hankies like the designer, Cynthia Rowley, did in 1999. Hankies can be framed and hung in arrangements on a wall; they're less expensive than paintings or prints and can be a far more personal way of expressing yourself. We often use hankies as table decorations at luncheons and dinners by filling vases with a bouquet of hankies instead of fresh flowers. This way, you get the color and vibrancy of a floral arrangement at no cost! For a recent birthday luncheon, we put a hanky in every wine glass. The hankies were carefully chosen to fit the personality of each of the women who attended and not only enlivened the table, but functioned as party favors. By contrast, for a wedding shower we folded white lace hankies into triangles and wrapped each with a lavendar ribbon. We placed them in a silver tray which we passed around the room, and each guest selected one to take home as a keepsake. For Christmas last year, we decorated a fellow collector's Christmas tree with Christmas hankies and pinned hankies to a clothesline strung around the room to create a garland effect. Think of an occasion and, with a little imagination, you'll come up with endless ways to decorate with hankies.

Christmas decoration.

Society uses of hankies.

Handkerchief skirts.

Storage in pizza boxes.

Hankies decorating wine glasses.

Hankies decorating wine glasses.

Lipstick hankies used in place settings.

White hankies in a silver basket as bridal shower favors.

Bunches of floral hankies create a center bouquet.

Chair pillows with hankies sewn on.

Clothesline wih hankies, good for parties.

Baskets of hankies as take-home gifts.

Poodle-themed hankies decorate a bathroom.

French-themed hankies decorate the bedroom of a French country house.

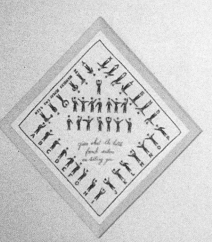

French-themed hankies decorate the bedroom of a French country house.

Hallways covered with French-themed hankies.

Hallways covered with French-themed hankies.

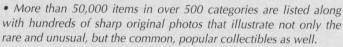

Bon Voyage